MAKING LIFE'S PUZZLE PIECES FIT

Using The Twelve Principles
of Personal Leadership

Greg L. Thomas

This book was printed in the United States of America.

To order additional copies of this book, contact:
Xlibris Corporation
1-888-795-4274
www.Xlibris.com
Orders@Xlibris.com
54457

Dedications & Acknowledgements

To my wife of thirty-four years, whose enduring love and personal example of caring are a continual inspiration to me. BJ, I love you with all my heart.

To my three daughters . . . Kelly, Karyn and Kathleen. I am very proud of you, and your accomplishments.

A special thanks to my son-in-law Joe Mango for his outstanding editing skills to greatly improve the quality of this book.

To my step-father and late mother. I can never thank you enough for the love, values and work ethic you taught me as a child.

To Ambassador College and Bellevue University for teaching me to love the foundation of knowledge, and the value of learning.

A special thanks to Karyn Thomas Standering for her excellent skills as a graphic artist in both my previous book and in this one. I also want to thank Kathleen Thomas and Joe Horton for spending many hours proof-reading and editing this book.

CONTENTS

INTRODUCTION

I am proud to introduce to you *Making Life's Puzzle Pieces Fit: Using The Twelve Principles of Personal Leadership.* In 1968, I discovered a magazine in a barber shop while waiting to get my hair cut. Inside the magazine was an advertisement for a free booklet entitled *The Seven Laws of Success.* Though I was only a teenager, this simple booklet changed my life forever. It was only fifty-six pages long, and some of the "laws" were briefly discussed in a few paragraphs. Nevertheless, the concepts behind the seven laws were powerful and had a profound effect on me. This booklet has been out of print for many years, but I'll never forget the impact it had on me at an impressionable young age.

It has been about fifty years since *The Seven Laws of Success* was first published. The world has changed greatly over that period of time, and I have come to see that there are *additional* essential principles needed not only to achieve and maintain success but also to attain personal fulfillment. It is my hope that the valuable information provided in this book will stir the hearts of the next generation to believe that they too can reach their greatest potential.

I actually first conceived this book back in 1992, and a close friend of mine who is now a weLEAD board member helped me to create these principles under a different title. However, at the time we had very few marketing dollars, and regrettably it was before the powerful influence of today's Internet. By 1993, we allowed the publication of these principles to lapse until 2004.

This book was primarily written for three important reasons. The first reason is because many people today struggle to make sense out of life. In our daily existence, positive living may appear to be a complex dance, and many people feel they are always out of step with the music. We actually make it more complicated than it was originally intended or needs to be. The truth is that millions of hard working people struggle to find their purpose in this world, and even fewer ever find *deep* personal fulfillment. The *Twelve*

Principles outlined in this book will bring all the fragments of life together to make a complete whole.

The second important reason this book was written is to encourage leadership development. This world needs more leaders, but not the counterfeit type we see far too often in our media. I call them the anti-leaders. The twelve principles within this book are built upon a single truth, which is that all real leadership starts from the *inside* out. The kind of leaders our society needs to solve its most perplexing and complicated problems are those whose values are based on solid bedrock moral beliefs. These are individuals who know and understand that leadership is a *calling* and an opportunity to leave their world or community or organization a better place than they found it. Leadership isn't about them; it is about contributing to the growth of others and gaining fulfillment through service and achievement.

The way either genuine leaders or anti-leaders act is simply a reflection of what is going on inside their hearts and minds. It reveals their true beliefs and values. *The Twelve Principles* tap into and expose this inner core, revealing that one has either the heart of genuine leadership or the cold-calculated mind of a harmful *anti*-leader.

I believe these twelve principles are *universal,* and I propose that the greatest individuals in human history—those who achieved remarkable, positive and truly lasting achievements—adhered to most of these principles either by conscious choice or by chance. A select few of the greatest servant-leaders in history lived by all of them.

Some of these principles have been discussed by outstanding authors such as Stephen Covey, Peter Block, Garry Wills, and others. I hope to discuss these commonly understood principles with a fresh and readable approach. However, a few of these principles offer new approaches and concepts not thoroughly discussed by other authors. I could tell you what these *Twelve Principles* are now, but I won't do that. I would rather reveal them one at a time like opening a series of gifts. I believe they will have more of an impact on your life that way!

The third major reason this book was written is to respond to a phenomenal change that is occurring in our modern society. It is the role of "followers" and their ability to now choose who or what they will respond to or follow. The major reason for this change is independent choice. In ancient times, the only real option one had was to dutifully follow the leader or die. However, in Western cultures, people who don't like their political leaders vote for others. People who don't like their jobs find other ones or consciously reduce their efforts on the job. People who are unhappy with their religious heritage end their association and move on. Attitudes are also slowly changing in non-Western cultures. What does all of this mean for the modern leader? It means followers now have a *choice* to support who or what they believe is best. No longer will most followers accept a win/lose relationship with the leaders getting what they want at the expense of the followers. Yes, people are still willing to be followers, especially for a good or noble cause. However, followers now expect and demand more from those in leadership positions. They expect their leaders to care for them, treat them with dignity, act responsibly and help them meet *their* needs. Any leader or organization who fails to do these things will soon meet with an exodus of followers. As leadership author John Maxwell states, "If you think you are leading and no one is following, you are only taking a walk!" This modern degree of skepticism has been caused by generations of poor leadership and abuse of power. There is one exception to this fact. Followers are still willing to blindly submit (for a while) to an autocratic culture for deeply personal, religious or philosophical reasons. But even in this case they have less tolerance today because of a clear history of mediocre and destructive leadership.

Are people still willing to follow good leaders? Yes, but they now have greater expectations and different roles. Followers are waiting for a *new* breed of leadership that understands they are a precious untapped resource. They are looking for leaders and missions that allow them *ownership* in the greater cause and help them to reach their own individual goals. They are looking for leaders they can trust, admire, respect and follow with pride rather than shame. Educator Joseph Rost sums it up well when he opines:

> Followers and leaders develop a relationship wherein they influence one another as well as the organization and society, and that is leadership. They do not do the same things in the relationship, just as the composers and musicians do not do the same thing in making music, but they are both essential to leadership.

The *real* problem is that good followers are fewer and often less committed because past abuse has persuaded many to become independent, uncommitted observers. Some have also become observers because they attempted to follow a mediocre leader and grew tired of waiting for positive things to happen. What does this mean for leadership in general? It means the leader must work harder than ever before to inspire, motivate and encourage a larger number of observers to make a personal commitment and become loyal supporters. This can only be done when a leader demonstrates integrity, self-sacrifice, dedication, and respect for the uncommitted observer as well as their current followers. As author Garry Wills comments, "Followers judge leaders. Only if the leaders pass that test do they have any impact." At no other time in history, have the roles of leaders and followers been more complex and challenging. Yet the truth remains that one of the best ways to grow into a great leader is to *first* become a great follower.

To lead others and lead well, you must understand and develop certain vital principles of what I call *personal leadership* to ensure you have the right traits, skills, and motives to produce positive and constructive results. What do I mean when I use this term? Personal leadership means to choose to seize control of your life and your own path. It means to stop allowing others, time, chance, or your culture to make your decisions for you. Personal leadership means you reject the *default* mission statement that your culture provides and choose one for yourself. To lead yourself or others is to accept responsibility and wisely determine your own future.

Maintaining personal leadership is indispensable if we desire to lead our families, our communities, our business organizations or our social institutions. Leadership isn't easy; it is often likened to "walking in a minefield." But it is easier, and the results are more productive, when we have the right *inner* compass to provide direction and purpose. This is why I believe that reading *Making Life's Puzzle Pieces Fit: Using The Twelve Principles of Personal Leadership* may be a life-altering experience.

Greg L. Thomas

#1
The Right
Visionary Goals

PRINCIPLE #1

THE RIGHT VISIONARY GOALS

Through the ages many people have dreamed about making the world a better place. If you are like this, you too may have wondered how you can help to change our world, especially when we see all the suffering and misery around much of the globe. Perhaps you have felt that there is something you can do. You may have even wondered how you can *lead* positive change. Most people make the terrible mistake of thinking that money or material possessions will magically give them the influence or power needed to become a leader. In this book you will begin to see that great leadership begins on the inside, is inspired by a deep desire to serve others, and then grows outwardly to create beneficial change. This is the kind of leadership that can powerfully change the world.

Right Visionary Goals

What is a goal? We can find out the definition of a goal by opening a dictionary and reading its meaning. It will tell us that a goal is an "aim" or an "objective." But a goal is much more than just an aim or objective because when goals are properly developed, they become guiding forces that motivate us toward greater personal accomplishment. They can give us the ability to accomplish new feats which may have never been done before. They also have the remarkable ability to change us forever. Goals can become essential tools that provide direction to our lives. This happens when our goals become a clear *reflection* of our own values.

I grew up in Cleveland, Ohio, and was privileged to be raised in a stable family. My relatives were hard working people, but the concept of establishing goals for their lives was not understood. Most of them simply graduated from high school and looked for a job in the local newspaper or got a tip from a friend that a factory was hiring. Their careers were not planned by goals, but by which company was hiring and paying good wages. In a similar way they had broad goals for life, such as "to buy a house," but most of the time they responded to events that occurred to them rather than choosing to plan for their own futures. When I was introduced to the importance of goal-setting and developing a personal vision, it changed my life. Since most young people and adults I have met still don't practice this principle, I have included it as the first.

The title of this chapter is "The Right Visionary Goals." Let's break down its meaning to understand it clearly. First, a *right* goal is one of benefit to ourselves *and* others. It is something we desire that is productive and fulfilling. However, if a goal is a benefit to ourselves at the expense or exploitation of others, it is a misguided goal. Therefore, we must candidly ask ourselves what the real motives are for our goals. If our desires are genuine, ethical and constructive, they are right goals. If our desires are to hurt, control or harm others, they are flawed.

Secondly, our goals must be visionary because it takes vision to have the steady perseverance needed to achieve our long-term goals over time. Forming a vision is a far different task than simply establishing our goals. Goals are the end result of a *course of action* that achieves something we deeply desire to accomplish, whereas vision is the mental picture that prods or inspires us to get there. This vision is the inspirational snapshot of a future we hold dear in our hearts which helps us overcome barriers or to continue when all appears to be lost. Vision reminds us of why the goal is important and worth struggling for. It is said that within the human mind, perception is reality. Vision is what we perceive and believe about the future and what it can be like.

Analogies to Consider

Visionary goals are those that we will *empower* by writing them down on paper. Almost all people have goals that are undefined. Most just have goals that are vague or nebulous, the "I'd like to do that someday" type. These are goals that will never be achieved. People often tell me that they have goals but I remind them that an unwritten goal is only a dream, and a goal without vision is only a fantasy.

Allow me to give you an analogy to explain why it is important to write down our goals and have a plan to achieve them. It's the analogy of a farmer planting seed. If a farmer wants to sow seed and have an abundant crop, he has to properly plant the seed. Without using good seed and the proper planting method, he won't have the successful, prosperous crop he desires. On the other hand, what would happen if he only *meant* to plant the seed someday? Or what happens if he doesn't prepare the field for planting and simply takes a handful of seed and throws it randomly on the hard ground? How much of a crop do you think he will reap? Sadly, he will both sow and reap a crop failure.

The same is true of our lives. We must begin with a visionary goal, prepare to articulate the goal, plan on how to achieve the goal by writing it down and methodically nurture it into an accomplishment. When you and I write down our goals, we empower them on paper so that we can read them, review them, and remember their importance. By doing this, we properly plant the mental "seeds" of commitment. Just like it's important for the farmer to plant his seed at the right *depth* into the soil, writing down our goals visually implants them in the depths of our hearts and minds. Then they can grow from being "someday dreams" to real achievements over the course of time.

If you were building a home, you would want that home to be built to the highest standards of quality. Assuming you wanted every wall and ceiling in that home to fit together properly, you would expect it to be designed with the aid of a set of architectural blueprints. These blueprints are the designer's vision of what the real home will look like. You wouldn't allow the builder to come in and say, "Well, I think we'll just throw up a wall over here. And let's just stop the wall right here and start installing the floor." If homes were constructed like that, they would be disorganized, dysfunctional and outright dangerous. Yet, unfortunately, many people plan and live their entire lives this way. Just as it is important to design "blueprints" for the proper building of a home, it is equally important that we design our future by committing our goals to paper. This in turn will help us to build our dreams into real accomplishments. Being committed to visionary goals written on paper is the blueprint of your future. They are what will give you direction and greater focus. Writing them down helps you to design your *desired* future. They provide us with the motivation and intensity to achieve the awesome potential we all possess.

Personal Mission Statement

However, before you begin to write down even a single goal, there is something far more important for you to create and put in writing. That is a *personal mission statement*. This is the step that many people skip, and by doing so they set themselves up for disappointment. Why am I delaying the discussion about our individual goals and turning toward a discussion of your personal life mission? We can't put the proverbial "cart before the horse." Our goals must be aligned with our personal mission statement. If they conflict with or contradict one another, frustration can be the result. As Stephen Covey has said, goals are invented to make your personal mission statement happen. Covey also uses the analogy of a ladder leaning against the wall. The wall is our personal mission in life. The ladder represents our individual goals to reach our mission. If the ladder is leaning against the *wrong* wall, it doesn't matter how high you climb! The most important thing we can do is first create our personal mission statements. Then we can create our individual life goals, making sure they are aligned together. We want to make sure the ladder is leaning against the right wall.

If you have not previously created your own personal mission statement, we will do it now before writing down your individual visionary goals. What is a mission statement? It is a term borrowed from the business world. Business today is complex and vulnerable. Any organization that wishes to survive must have a clear "mission statement" and an unquenchable drive to achieve it. A mission statement for a business describes the purpose of the organization and outlines the types of activities to be performed for constituents and customers. It should also mention what unique value or services the organization offers as a *byproduct* of its work.

Our lives can be very complicated in today's modern world. To maximize our individual potential and opportunities, we must have a "personal mission statement." What is yours? In a *special* way your personal mission statement will define your purpose in this world along with the major goals and values you seek to achieve. It is your own particular "constitution" that reflects your unique life mission and moral standards. It will help to focus your energies and resources. It will also provide a sense of orientation and unify the fragments of your life. If you haven't created one yet, please do so now before you write down even a single individual goal. If you already have a personal mission statement, this may be a good time to review it against the model outlined below.

Why should you create or review your personal mission statement right now? Here are some important points to ponder:

1. It defines what you value. (Moral compass.) This is a great aid, particularly during difficult times in life when your ethics or standards are under assault.
2. What do you stand for? (Belief system.) This includes deeply held principles, including your degree or level of spirituality.

3. What is your essential or primary mission in life? If you have yet to articulate your own essential mission, the process of creating your personal mission statement will stimulate you to meditate on this essential question.

4. What are your responsibilities? Many people ultimately fail because they either forget their personal responsibilities to others or falsely believe they are "above" the normal expectations required of others.

Here are some things to remember when creating your personal mission statement. It is yours only and is not meant to please anyone else. Personalize it for yourself. This is *your* special assignment and is a unique creation. Take the time to ask yourself some heartfelt questions and articulate some clear responses. Your personal mission statement is supposed to be *different* than everyone else's.

Make it as short or as long as you want. There is not a "hard and fast" rule on its length, but if you want to frame it to hang on a wall, it will need to be succinct to be readable in limited space. Be patient and work on it until it *inspires* you. The idea is for this document to motivate you when it is referred to in the future. It is a written reminder of who you say you are and what your life is all about.

It should reflect not just the way you are today, but what you hope to become in a *preferred* future. Remember that leaders are visionaries who seek to improve themselves and the world they live in. How would you like your world to become better and more fulfilling for yourself and others?

Putting Pen to Paper

What are the vital steps to creating your own personal mission statement? When sitting down to write your mission statement, remember that it should be composed of at least four basic parts. If it is too short, the statement will be ambiguous and have very little real meaning. (Some organizations suffer from the same problem.) On the other hand, if it is too long, it will lose its motivational impact and read like a journal. Four to five paragraphs is a good, readable length.

Here are the *four* basic parts I recommend be included as part of your document:

Part 1—Your beliefs and values—what is your purpose in life and what are the moral and ethical values you live by.

Part 2—Your personal family goals—including as a parent, spouse, and relationships with other family members.

Part 3—Your personal career goals—why you work, what is your career's purpose, and what skills need to be developed.

Part 4—Your personal life goals—the importance of education, spiritual development, expanding your talents, maintaining health, and loving others in your personal life.

Here are some more details on what each of these parts can include:

Your beliefs and values. What is your moral code? What values give guidance to your daily life? Is it the "golden rule," religious Scriptures or another source? This is where you should begin. In this opening paragraph of your mission statement, strongly state your deeply held ethical principles and moral code. If you haven't thought intensely about this before, it could be the most *revealing* part of your mission statement. Let your heart talk to you.

Your personal family goals. This includes close relationships with your parent(s), spouse, children and/or extended family. If you want a happy and balanced family life, you also need to have these essential goals. Of course, receiving input from all family members will make these goals more attainable and fun to achieve. How do you want to "coach" and encourage each member to become all they can possibly be?

Your personal career goals. Why do you work? Is it to find personal fulfillment or simply to generate income for other interests in life? Do you want to change your career path? If so, how do you plan on making this change? Are there career skills you want to enhance or acquire? At the end of your career, what do you want others to say about your contribution in the workplace?

Your personal life goals. This part includes some of the most satisfying aspects of human life, and sadly most people put these off until retirement or forever. How do you plan on *maintaining* a healthy body and mind? Do you need more education to fulfill a lifelong personal goal? Do you desire to "give back" to others for the blessings you have been granted? What would you do for the rest of your life if money was *not* a limitation?

If you have never before created your own personal mission statement, I suggest that you first finish reading this book completely and then sit down in a quiet environment to construct it. Don't rush the process; let your creativity express what is in your mind. Allow this document to be a vital *extension* of you. Take pride and ownership in what you write. If you get a feeling of mental gridlock, step away for a few hours and come back to it later. Work on it until the document reflects what you truly feel and believe. Allow your personal mission statement to inspire you.

Once you have completed a personal mission statement and are ready to write down your individual visionary goals in more detail, be aware of some common mistakes to goal setting.

Common Mistakes

One common mistake is that many people establish goals that are just too overwhelming. An improperly defined goal can seem so large that we become discouraged by looking at its immensity. If you have a single goal which is too large, one that seems like you're "reaching for the moon," you are going to become de-motivated. It is natural to lose all personal incentive and motivation to achieve a goal that appears impossible or unachievable. Don't worry though; soon I'm going to tell you how to make that seemingly large impossible goal a reality.

Another common mistake is that many people do not understand the importance of creating both long-term goals *and* short-term goals. They usually begin by "jotting down" a long-term life achievement goal. Some individuals write down a large vague target without thinking about how they are ever going to get there. The process of accomplishing a major goal is usually a lengthy journey. Many folks don't understand the important *interaction* between long-term goals and short-term goals and why it's necessary to have both! It's not enough to simply create a list of your goals. If done improperly, you may subliminally convince yourself they are unattainable. Larger goals can only be effective if you dissect your long-term goals by creating a series of short-term goals.

Both Short-term and Long-term Goals Are Necessary

Observe how a farmer prepares for a successful season. He goes through several *stages* to get the most out of his fields. He tills the land, fertilizes the soil, and plants more seeds than will sprout to ensure a good crop. Then the farmer nurtures the plants, maintains the equipment, and finally cultivates the harvest. He knows that these steps are all important to reach his goal of an abundant crop. Our goals also need to be organized, planted, nurtured and cultivated with a "step by step" approach.

A long-term goal is one we establish for ourselves that normally takes years and great effort to achieve. Sometimes five years, ten years, twenty years, or perhaps even a lifetime. These long-term goals are the major objectives that you want to achieve in your life. Now how do our short-term goals interact with these major objectives? Short-term goals are the smaller targets or "stepping stones" which we establish to achieve these long-term objectives. Each short-term goal leads us toward the direction of our larger goals because they are a smaller part (or piece) of a bigger goal.

Short-term goals are the "rungs of a ladder" we climb to reach a long-term objective at the top of the ladder. These short-term goals are usually established for a period from a few days to perhaps a few years. We detail this by writing a goal with a major heading followed by the short-term goals that will achieve it. Here our major heading is our first long-term goal. So write down something like "I desire to." This goal should be your *highest* priority and of greatest personal importance in your life. Again, as I mentioned earlier, this goal may be something different for each of us. Begin to think about it now and start to commit it to writing. Now ask yourself this important question. Is this goal aligned with my personal mission statement? If not, at least one of them is flawed. Envision why this goal is important to you. Picture in your mind how it would feel to have this goal completed and accomplished.

I encourage you to write down your major goals in order of *priority*. The first should be the most important long-term goal you have, and following this heading, the short-term goals or steps you will take to accomplish it. Next, write down the second most important long-term goal and the necessary short-term goals or steps to achieve it. Do this for three or four major goals. I also want to encourage you to stay focused. Don't distract yourself by making your goals too elaborate or lengthy. It is not necessary to write a "thesis" to explain your hopes and desires. A well thought out paragraph is fine. Make sure you *focus* on what you truly desire.

Life is a Process of Change

Another subject we need to understand is that our goals are going to *change* throughout our lifetimes. This maturing process is normal and natural. Some of the goals you have at twenty years old will *not* be the same goals you will have at age thirty-five. This will continue as you age. Yes, some essential values and goals should remain fixed throughout life, like some spiritual or family obligations. But we need to recognize that life is meant to be a maturing and changing process.

As you grow older and your perceptions or circumstances change, you are going to find that previous goals you once thought were very important are not considered important any more. When this happens, seek to understand why, and reevaluate the importance of these goals. You should occasionally read aloud your goals in a private setting. They should have the same meaning and importance that they had when originally created. However, every year it is a good idea to privately sit down and reevaluate all the goals you previously established. Ask yourself: Is this goal still important to me? Am I focusing on the *right* ones or expending energies on an objective that is no longer important? You will discover there are times when you actually eliminate a goal which is no longer of value or may have been totally achieved. At the same time, also review your smaller accomplishments to encourage and motivate yourself. Remember, these changes are healthy and normal due to life experiences and ripening wisdom. Don't allow yourself to become discouraged at the need for change. Some of the desires and material possessions that *seem* so important to you now will most likely change as you gracefully mature with age and experience.

Remember that our goals must be aligned with our personal mission statements. If they conflict with or contradict one another, the result can be unhappiness or failure. Be sure your ladder is leaning against the right wall.

What is Real Failure?

So what happens when you fail to meet a goal? It just may be a stepping stone to success in *another* direction. We have several options or choices when this happens. The first option, obviously, is to keep trying to reestablish the goal with increased commitment. The second option is to modify what we originally desired. Ask yourself whether that goal was really important to you. Is the goal truly aligned with our stated personal mission statement? If you feel it is, keep trying, go forward, and don't look back with regrets. It has become history and is now in the past. We can't change the past. You and I can only change our tomorrows. We can become masters of our own destiny by doing something today that will change tomorrow's outcome, but we can't do anything about yesterday. The third option we have is to eliminate the goal entirely if it is flawed or no longer of value.

Don't become discouraged if you decide to change or eliminate a goal. Instead, look at *other* new possibilities that may have been revealed in the process. Think of the lessons you learned. Reflect on a few important things you *did* achieve. Meditate on the personal and individual growth you were able to develop in the process of striving toward that goal. By no means look at yourself as a failure. Never forget that perceived failure is often success when seen from a different point of view.

We are in large part *masters* of our own destiny, but we are also subject to unforeseen circumstances. Time and chance can prevent or delay us from achieving some of our major goals. There are often situations in life which are beyond our control. It may be a personal tragedy, or you may experience a period of depression. It may be a natural tragedy or a personal handicap. You may be faced with the death of a loved one or be in the midst of a difficult personal relationship with another. When these tragedies or events happen, they are clearly "time and chance" circumstances that may prevent or delay us from achieving a goal. Don't give up, but go forward and keep trying to accomplish your goals. Allow yourself a period of time to naturally mourn or grieve over personal tragedy. Then redouble your efforts to successfully achieve your goals. Also, remember to be patient with yourself. Good things, like fine wine, take time and patience. Winston Churchill sometimes suffered from periods of deep discouragement in his life, yet his bulldog determination is legendary. In spite of his personal episodes of melancholy, Churchill reached deep down inside himself to remain committed and optimistic about winning the Second World War.

HI-PAY vs. LO-PAY Pursuits

How can you better organize your time? As I mentioned earlier, there just isn't enough time for us to do all the things we want to accomplish. How effectively we use our time basically boils down to recognizing two different *lifestyle* activities. The first type is what I call "HI-PAY" pursuits. These are *high* payoff activities that are directly related to our goals. They are pursuits that we can't delegate or ask someone else to do for us. Quite often they are activities that are rather unpleasant. Typically they are at a higher risk level and are the more difficult activities in life.

On the other hand, all of us also have a secondary type of lifestyle activity I call "LO-PAY" pursuits. These are *low* payoff activities usually not related to any of our goals. We may feel they are important, but they really offer us little in return. They are comfortable, oftentimes uncreative, and perhaps trivial. They typically have simply become a routine in our lives. These are activities that present little challenge or risk whatsoever. Many of these LO-PAY pursuits are habits we have acquired over the years which now serve no real purpose.

Here's the way to focus more intently on your goals: begin to eliminate some of these *low* payoff pursuits by learning to say "no" to unimportant or unproductive activities. We begin this by mentally evaluating and separating the importance of our HI-PAY from our LO-PAY pursuits. High payoff activities that are related to our jobs, to our families, and to our goals should be *most* important to us. We must learn to say "no" to low payoff pursuits and not feel guilty for setting priorities in our lives.

Here's an interesting philosophy for you to think about: People without goals are often used by people who have them. Think about this deeply, and you will discover it is true. People who have direction in life, those who have goals and are deeply motivated with purpose in their lives, are the ones who lead the masses of people who have no goals or real direction. It's the leader and follower principle. In almost any society, you will find that the *goal setters* (such as business entrepreneurs, political, military, and religious leaders) are the "movers and shakers" of any society.

Recap of Principle #1

Don't forget the importance of establishing visionary written goals for your life. Spend some quiet time to get this done. Doing this is the bedrock foundation of the other principles we will discuss. I encourage you to *choose* the most important things in life to you. Focus your thinking on HI-PAY pursuits and on the very *people* who are most important in your life. You can choose to affect your own destiny. Establish right visionary goals, not by just dreaming about them, but by committing them to writing. Create both short-term and long-term goals, and dedicate a certain amount of time each day to the achievement of these goals. Understand that our interests and goals are going to change throughout our lives. There will be times when you decide to change or eliminate a goal, and that is natural. Unfortunately, *time and circumstance* may prevent us from achieving important goals we have established, but we can choose to continue them at a later time if we desire.

Establishing the right visionary goals will change your life. Leaders are goal *setters* and goal accomplishers. Get started right now. We will be discussing some of these insights in greater detail throughout the rest of this book.

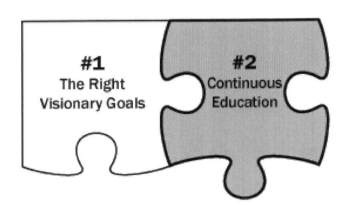

PRINCIPLE #2

<u>CONTINUOUS EDUCATION</u>

Education is one of the great pleasures and necessities of a rich, abundant life. To reach our fullest human potential, we need to understand the importance and lifelong value of a complete education. I am not only talking about our formal education but also a lifetime of constructive, continuous learning. The traditional view of education is that of a formal institutional program taught in schools and universities. A more complete definition is that education is a *lifelong* process which includes our formal education plus experiences gained from human relationships, family and lifestyle choices. These "real-life" activities exert a greater influence and occupy more time than formal schooling.

Growing up in Cleveland, I would say we were a middle class family, but our neighborhood was on the edge of a declining section of the city. For this reason I was assigned to one of the worst high schools in the city of Cleveland. The school building was old, and it had the atmosphere of a prison. We didn't even have a track, or baseball and football fields. As a member of the track team, I practiced running around a parking lot where they had spread gravel. It took eleven laps to equal a mile. The administration could never figure out why we never won a track meet. The school also suffered from constant racial problems due to students being bused from another part of the city. Many of the teachers at the school were poorly trained, and they either didn't care or didn't know how to motivate young people.

As a teenager, I was not motivated to excel in high school and did not receive a good education. At the time of my graduation from high school, I didn't realize how much of a disadvantage I had compared to others who attended better schools. It took me the next seven years to catch up to where I should have been all along. I learned the hard way about the significance of receiving a good formal education.

Most people end their formal education upon graduation from high school, college or vocational school. But think about this fact: We have the most educated population in the history of humankind. Many Western nations have made unbelievable achievements in the elimination of illiteracy among their peoples. Even the third world nations have made impressive advances in the reduction of illiteracy. Yet, with all of these strides in formal education, we still see great misery, violence and frustration in many of these same nations, among so-called educated peoples. Why? As I heard one college chancellor state, "Young people are being taught how to make a living, but not how to live."

What is Education?

Education is not a venture that ends in our mid-twenties upon receiving a degree or diploma. Proper education should be an exciting lifelong pursuit. Here's what Thomas Jefferson wrote about this pursuit in a letter he wrote in 1786:

> Ever in our power, always leading us to something new, never cloying, we ride, serene and sublime, above the concerns of this mortal world, contemplating truth and nature, matter and motion, the laws which bind up their existence, and that Eternal being who made and bound them up by these laws. Let this be our employ.

Notice the *zeal* he had to acquire more knowledge of the world around him. To Jefferson, education was an exciting adventure, and he pursued it with a passion. Within his lifetime he was an accomplished lawyer, statesman, politician, author, inventor, botanist, architect and educator. How have you viewed the importance of education in your life? To examine the importance of education, we need to view this pursuit as two different aspects. The first is our "formal" education, and the second is what we will call our informal or continuing educational process.

Allow me to give you a brief example of how we can benefit from a continuing educational process. In a previous paragraph I quoted Thomas Jefferson, and within his statement he used the word *cloying* as in his phrase "never cloying." Did you catch the word and do you know what it means? Did you gloss over it and hope to determine what it means by guessing the context? I certainly didn't know its meaning the first time I read this statement. It's the descendant of an Old English word which means "excessive to the point of being distasteful." Jefferson loved knowledge and was passionate about the study of science and nature, but not to the point of excess by excluding his other personal responsibilities.

When ordinary people come across a word they are not familiar with or do not understand, they usually ignore it or guess at its meaning by the message's content. However, when you understand the importance of your lifelong educational experience, these unknown words are valuable new discoveries! Begin to take the time to expand your world. When you discover a word you don't understand, open a dictionary and find out about a powerful fresh word which can help you to express your thoughts more deeply.

Importance of a Complete Education

I am sure that you have heard of the proverbial three "R's" of education as being reading, w(r)iting and a(r)ithmetic. Our culture and educational systems need to immediately add *two* other R's to our formal educational institutions. These additional R's are the disciplines of *reasoning* and *responsibility*. Neither of these essential traits can simply be taught in a book. They used to be primarily taught in the home and in our religious institutions; but since the breakdown of both of these traditional structures has occurred, a tremendous void has been created in our modern educational systems. We will discuss these two additional R's to a greater degree later in this chapter. However, let's first talk about the importance of achieving a sound formal education.

One of the most positive attributes of modern civilization has been to provide a means of education for its people. Education is personal freedom. The ability to read and write gives people a window to brave new worlds and opportunities they would otherwise never experience. A balanced and advanced formal education is one of the greatest gifts any person can ever receive. If you have been blessed to receive one, you are a privileged member of an earthly minority.

Do you remember the analogies we discussed in the first principle about establishing proper goals? We used the analogy of a farmer planting his seed and how important it is for the farmer to use the proper planting methods to insure an abundant crop. A successful farmer knows he must be educated in the field of crop management. He understands the value of learning about effective planting methods as well as learning about productive soil and weather conditions. He prepares to be successful. How about you? Have you prepared through education to be successful in your life and career? Do you have the complete education needed to achieve your goals?

Another analogy we used previously was that of building a home. I mentioned how our goals are the "blueprints" of how we construct our future. After the "blueprints" are complete, the next important step is to locate educated craftsmen to actually build the structure. It requires knowledgeable and skilled individuals to properly design and build a home. In the same way, it will require skill and educational development for you to achieve your goals. Any goals you establish are incomplete unless you have the education required to accomplish them. Even if you are able to achieve them without the education needed, a gross lack of knowledge will make you vulnerable to losing all you have accomplished by neglect or faulty decision-making.

What do I mean when I say you need a *complete* education? This is an education that develops the whole person. A complete education includes formal subject studies, self-discipline, personality and character development. Many people in our modern world receive a formal education but lack the development of personality, character or self-discipline. This eventually leads to their demise. As an example, look at our entertainment and sports industries. Some athletes and performers who receive adequate formal educations and work hard at their craft find quick success. But in time they lose it all, because of a lack of character or self-discipline. A complete education recognizes the absolute importance of developing the entire mind, body and personality with a focus on fulfilling your purpose.

Here's my main point regarding a complete education: it's highly important to be properly educated in order to reach your intended goals as we discussed in principle number one. Education is the preparation or *know-how* you acquire to reach your goals one step at a time. We can't reach our goals through instinct like other animals; we have to be taught to think, reason, design, plan and build. We need to be educated in order to be prepared for what we intend to do with our lives. And after we achieve our goals, education helps us to maintain them.

Education Beyond the Classroom

Don't stop educating yourself simply because you have earned a degree or diploma. As Jefferson said, education is a lifelong pursuit. Keep sharp and always challenge or *stretch* yourself. Take a few classes at your local college or vocational school. Use these activities to expand your world and your mind. Classroom settings are great environments for personal growth. Learning, much like exercising, is easier when shared with others and performed regularly.

Again, education includes not only a *formal* education, but also a lifelong quest to further one's knowledge and understanding of the world around us. Our formal education usually ends in our twenties, but for those who desire a more meaningful future, a far greater degree of real world education must continue for us to be successful.

This continuing education needs to literally become a part of your lifestyle. Too many people allow falling in the "rut" of their daily existence to stunt any further real education in their lives. They never expand their world or their knowledge of it. Their free time becomes primarily involved in self-entertainment rather than personal enlightenment or self-development.

Please don't misunderstand me. We all need generous amounts of recreation and entertainment to enjoy a balanced life. These enjoyable and refreshing activities are important needs. A later principle of *personal leadership* will discuss one's absolute need to maintain balance through recreational pursuits. However, many adults have allowed their minds to stagnate to the point of intellectual numbness. The human mind can be set on "auto pilot" and will no longer want to stretch or expand. It will just desire to vegetate and drift if we are not careful. Millions of individuals now go through life allowing *others* opinions and values to be fed into their sedated minds by the modern media. Many come home day-after-day and sit in front of a television for hours, allowing a precious opportunity to learn and grow erode away. Don't allow this to happen to you. Again, there is nothing wrong with watching some television for relaxation or entertainment. It is how much we do so, and why, that is the question. Keep your mind sharp and expanding by being proactive about your learning. In the next paragraph are a few important ways to keep your mind active and alert. Remember, a truly informed person is a better decision-maker and is better prepared for success.

Begin to read widely. There is an old saying I was taught many years ago. An unread book is only a block of paper. A person who can read and doesn't is no better off than one who can't. Reading is educational, relaxing, and enlightening. Books, newspapers, and magazines should be a significant part of our lifestyle. Use these valuable tools to teach yourself about history, literature, the sciences, and responsible living. The potential reading list is endless. Read a variety of subjects that catch your interest, not just fiction or novels. Make reading a *passion* in your life. Begin to learn about all of those things you always wanted to know more about but never had the time to pursue. This activity is so important, that you should devote at least a half-hour a day to reading. If your lifestyle is such that this is impossible or if you are handicapped, perhaps the use of digital media devices, DVD's or Podcasts can help to fill this need. There are now thousands of digital audio programs for virtually every area of interest; including world news, languages, history and novels. You can now expand your mind while commuting, dressing for the day, relaxing at home or eating your lunch. And don't think that you need to spend lots of money to do this. The Internet or your local library probably has access to an unlimited number of these audio and video programs for you to download or borrow free of charge. Learn to use the resources of your local library or the Internet. Take time out from your busy schedule to use these modern resources often. Some of the *talk radio* programs that have intelligent moderators can also be a resource for stimulating thought and expanding knowledge.

I am reminded of a story *reputed* to have happened between Albert Einstein and a colleague. The colleague asked Einstein his telephone number. Albert proceeded to open a phone book and look up his own phone number. His colleague was amazed and said, "Albert, you are considered a genius and one of the greatest minds of the twentieth century. Why are you looking for your telephone number in the phone book?" Einstein is reputed to have replied, "I never memorize anything I can find in a book." This story may be fabled, but the moral of this story is that Einstein had learned the value of knowing where to find information rather than just memorizing it.

Living or Being Lived by Others

You need to keep your mind sharp and alert by being keenly aware of the world around you. If you do this, you will form your *own* opinions rather than having the media tell you what you are supposed to believe. When we allow our minds to coast and become influenced by talking heads, we are no longer really living on our own terms; we are allowing our values and ideas to be formed by others. When you are growing and aware of the world around you, it guides you to be proactive and in control of your own decisions. Watch the daily news to learn what's occurring in this vast world of ours. Remember, our world is much bigger than the community and surroundings we live in. Read a daily newspaper or watch a half-hour *world* news program once a day. Keep informed and abreast of world events. As a citizen of the planet and of a global community, you need to be concerned and know what's happening. Sooner or later it will affect your community, lifestyle or standard of living.

The Missing Two "R's"

Earlier I mentioned the valuable two "R's" missing from today's formal educational systems. These valuable traits are not missing because of a fault in modern education alone. After all, our educational institutions are just a *reflection* of the rest of our society and culture. I would now like to discuss these two traits in greater detail. As I do, ask yourself how well you apply these essential characteristics in your life.

The first missing "R" is *reasoning*. This is the ability to put bits of information together and make a reasoned conclusion leading to a good decision. A reasoned decision is one that contemplates *both* the positive and negative consequences of an action.

Much of our educational system still stresses Plato's emphasis on *intellectual absorption* of information. However, in an increasingly complex world, this intellectual knowledge is vastly limited without the development of rational decision-making skills and an understanding of the "cause and effect" principle. Not enough importance is being placed in young people's minds regarding the long-term effects of their decision-making. Greater stress must be placed on realizing the consequences of poor decision-making. We are no longer teaching the "cause and effect" principle which governs everyone's life. For every cause there *is* an effect. As a distorted society, we are falsely teaching that we can avoid the effects of bad decision-making by covering or masking the causes. This lack of sound reasoning is one of the major causes for increased drug usage, unwanted pregnancy and despondency among various people today. Our youth are being *lied* to by a dysfunctional culture that now tells them that a government program will solve their problems or that "redefining" a term or traditional institution will make everything come out all right.

The problem is that we are no longer stressing the essential trait of *reasoning* at virtually any level of society. Most of our families, schools and religious institutions are falling far short of their purpose and vital role to instill personal accountability. Modern Western governments are spending so much money and energy treating the effects of deep social and personal problems that we have ignored the *causes* of these problems.

How about you? Have you also been caught up in this environment? Do you make decisions in your business or family that seem to come back and *boomerang* upon you? Do you decide upon matters only to have them explode, leaving you with unintended consequences? The reason may be because you never really developed the skill of *reasoning* and have been making decisions based on a reaction or emotion. To control our own destiny and lead others, we must learn to reason soundly, and this requires a gathering of valid facts and serious contemplation of the consequences of our decisions. A personal study of what is called *systems theory* may help you to see why more clearly.

The Second "R"—Responsibility

The second missing "R" is also rapidly declining in both our formal institutions of education and within our culture. This trait goes *hand-in-hand* with reasoning. It is *responsibility*. The lack of taking personal responsibility for one's actions is a major cause of suffering and failure in our world. From the earliest ages of youth, we now say to individuals, "You are not responsible for your own conduct or actions." The message is that "you are a helpless victim." Many want you to believe that every problem is your parent's fault, or your doctor's fault, or your employer's fault, or your teacher's fault, or the fault of religion, or your environment. They declare, "It's *not* really your fault." This twisted philosophy now affects almost every aspect of our judicial and social institutions like a metastasized cancer. What proponents of this distorted philosophy have failed to realize is that it teaches helplessness and hopelessness. It says in effect that your actions are out of your control; that your life and conduct are manipulated and controlled by others. This belief is false and dangerous. To be successful and happy in life, you must accept responsibility for your own actions and decisions.

When you have the wisdom and courage to *accept* responsibility for your own actions, you are acknowledging control and accountability for your own life and destiny. Think about this fact, responsibility is not exclusively a moral or ethical principle. It is an *act* of self-discipline, and the very meaning of the word education is to "be disciplined." Yes, all of us have certainly been influenced by the past. Yes, our upbringing and peer groups have had a great influence on our personal development. However, to use negative life experiences as an excuse for our actions is self-defeating and deceptive. Don't sell yourself or your own abilities short. Stop the victimization "blame game" and start to take control of your thoughts and your life. We can't change yesterday, but what we do today can literally change our tomorrows. To be a great leader you must absolutely take responsibility for your conduct and actions, both good and bad.

Recap of Principle #2

Let's review some of the things we have discussed in this principle.

Education is really a two-step process in life. One step is our *formal* education, which begins in early childhood and continues until we are adults. However, we also discussed how a complete education should become a lifelong process or *quest* for personal growth and self-improvement. It will require skill and educational development for you to achieve your chosen and written goals. Any goals you establish are incomplete unless you have the education required to accomplish them.

It pays to receive a good *formal* education in today's complicated world. In our specialized society, college or technical training beyond high school is now a must. Depending on your skills and goals, your avenue to increased formal training may come through vocational schooling, college, or a trade school apprenticeship program.

In this chapter, you are encouraged to make education a vital part of your daily lifestyle. This includes *reading* widely and extensively to learn about the world around you. This habit will help you expand your personal interests and gain new resources.

Sadly, our educational systems are now reflecting other disintegrating social structures such as the home and our culture. This vacuum is causing an increased need to learn two additional "R's" and make them a part of your character. These are *reasoning* and *responsibility*.

I hope you can see that *continuing* education is not only essential for you to achieve your goals and personal leadership but also to maintain them. Many thousands of people have acquired temporary success only to lose it all because of a lack of a complete education, especially regarding the two "R's."

Great leadership is the kind that changes the world in a positive way and leaves it a better place. Developing personal leadership prepares you to become a great leader and to sustain your ability to lead. Education is a lifelong quest, which includes your formal training. But it more importantly includes what you have learned from your *informal* life experiences and your personal relationships with others. I encourage you to develop a complete education in the pursuit of excellence.

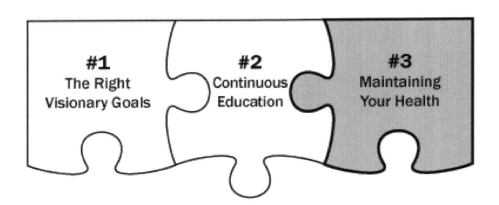

PRINCIPLE #3

<u>MAINTAINING YOUR HEALTH</u>

At age forty-nine, I found myself in the doctor's office hearing some very discouraging news. I had just completed an annual physical, and my white blood cell count was abnormally high. The next few weeks were terrifying as I discovered that I had a chronic blood disease! At first, we didn't know how fast it would progress, and if it did progress quickly, my blood count would rise so high it would cause serious health problems. Then I would be faced with some difficult medical decisions. Thankfully, it has been a number years since the diagnosis, and my blood count has changed so little it may not cause a problem for years to come, if ever. I am happy to report that I am feeling fine, but I learned a valuable lesson on how ill health can *immediately* change all of our hopes and plans.

Have you had a health "check-up" lately? What is your attitude about your health, and what does it have to do with personal leadership? Actually, what you think about your health reveals a lot about your leadership perspective. Some folks take their health for granted and think that they have little control over it. They believe there is a cosmic clock that is ticking, and "when your time is up," you die. They look at their time on earth as limited to a predetermined fate. Others believe that they have a certain amount of control over their health and have the ability to delay serious health issues. Which one is correct? It all boils down to your *locus of control,* and this will tell you a lot about yourself.

Locus of Control

Your *locus of control* is a "personality orientation" originally developed by Julian Rotter in the 1960s. Determining whether you have a strong *internal* or *external* orientation tells you a lot about yourself and may affect the way you view your health. Those who test and show a strong *internal* orientation tend to believe that life and its various events are determined more by their own actions than by uncontrollable forces or chance. This is an admirable quality in a manager or leader. They believe that what they do (or don't do) can make a difference in the workplace or the world. They don't view themselves as victims, and they tend to be more future-orientated. Folks with strong "internals" also feel confident that they have the power to influence others. When problems arise, they are less resistant to change in life, and respond with innovation and flexibility.

On the other hand, individuals with a strong *external* orientation believe that they have little opportunity to improve their lives. They tend to think that fate or chance mostly determines what happens in life. This is not an admirable trait in a manager or leader. These strong "externals" guide one to believe that much in life is out of their control. They tend to accept victimization as a way of life and lack aggressive goals because achieving them is felt to be beyond their control. They often feel that whatever they do (or don't do) doesn't really matter or make much of a difference. When problems arise, they typically don't respond quickly or effectively, and they are highly resistant to change.

Think about your personal *locus of control* and how this may influence your approach to health. Do you believe that your lifestyle and eating habits affect your quality of life? Do you think that having a positive outlook on life and your role in the world influences your physical health and well-being? If you do, you have the right perspective and attitude about your health. For a moment, just consider the thousands of talented individuals who worked hard for twenty or thirty years to climb to the top of their chosen professions only to lose it all because of destructive lifestyle habits or addictions.

Our DNA is Unique

In understanding our health, there are some things we have limited control over and things we have a large amount of control over. Let's begin to consider some of them.

One area where we have limited control is our genetic structure or DNA. We are all familiar with the term DNA, which is short for deoxyribonucleic acid. DNA is a nucleic acid that carries the genetic information in the cell and is capable of self-replication and synthesis of RNA (ribonucleic acid). DNA determines our individual hereditary characteristics. It is an important component in understanding our physiology. We are all the product of thousands of years of genetic mixture that makes us both truly unique and prone to physical strengths and weaknesses. Research is revealing that many health problems are common within families. The tendency or trait to have specific diseases is often inherited and passed down to the next generation.

Our own particular DNA can be either good or bad depending on the genetic tendencies. It is bad if we inherit the tendency to develop a specific disease. It can be good if it has a tendency toward good health and longevity. Some have jokingly remarked about how Winston Churchill reputedly smoked five cigars and drank a quart of brandy almost every day. However, he lived to be the ripe old age of ninety one. In his case, the fact that some of his ancestors lived to a ripe old age worked in his favor. On the other hand, Winston's father, Lord Randolph, was also a gifted man and a member of Parliament. Yet he abused his health and squandered his life. He died at age forty-six, reputedly from the ravages of a venereal disease.

The thing we need to understand is that even within our genetic structure we do have some flexibility and control. In most cases, genetics give us a tendency or increased risk toward a particular disease. Rarely does it absolutely guarantee we will acquire a disease. For example, I know that my father and most of his siblings died of various forms of cancer. This can alert me to the need for careful annual physicals and special attention to anything unusual going on in my body. Some close relatives died of cancers resulting from the habit of smoking, and this tells me that I should not even *consider* smoking since it has proven to shorten the lifespan of many individuals. Folks that have a family history of diabetes or high blood pressure can take steps to improve their health by noticing early warning signs. They can then modify their diets or take medications to control it. Understanding our genetic family trees can help us to stay on guard for potential diseases and take aggressive action when they are detected early.

Lifestyle Can Make a Difference

One area in which we can have enormous control over our health is in monitoring our daily lifestyle. The facts are very clear. What we eat, and how much food we consume, can have a significant impact on our quality of life and the development of chronic disease. Along with this, we should be concerned with exercise and possessing a positive mental outlook toward life. These are all areas in which we can have significant control and influence, but they take effort and commitment. Again, this goes back to our personal *locus of control.* If our personalities have strong internal orientations, we will tend to make changes and be proactive toward our health. If we have strong external orientations, we may allow "time and chance" to control us and our futures. What a tragedy to work so hard at the first two principles we have discussed only to let it all slip away due to negligence. We may work very hard to develop and seek the right visionary goals. We may then spend years growing in a continuous education to develop a great degree of personal leadership. However, if we take for granted or abuse our bodies, the result will be poor health. It is hard to lead or reach maximum potential when your mind is distracted with constant pain, anxiety or weariness.

Perhaps the greatest change that has occurred in the modern history of our Western world is the *lack* of physical activity. For thousands of years, exercise was a normal part of daily living. Activities such as farming, making crafts, or building were hard work and resulted in exertion, strengthening of muscles and cardio-vascular exercise. However, the *latter* part of the twentieth century brought about a whole new lifestyle for millions of individuals. It was the result of many new career roles such as supervisors, various office positions, retail sales, and other jobs in the service industry. Now many workers were given the sedentary work of communicating, analyzing and monitoring various activities, often from a desk and in front of a computer screen. Our bodies were designed to maintain internal strength through vigorous work and movement. The result of inactivity is a slow but insidious deterioration of our health.

Exercise properly stresses and tones our body so it can maximize its potential. I am not talking about lifting massive weights or "bulking up" on protein powders. We are talking about a *regular* exercise routine that pushes our hearts, lungs, circulatory systems and major muscle groups in order to strengthen them. The benefits of exercise are both short-term, and long-term, and they will likely improve our quality of life. Many excellent books have been written about the benefits of exercise and various types of exercises. It is not my goal to provide these specific details, but to convince you why exercise should be important to you. Once you begin, you will notice a marked improvement in your energy level and alertness through the day.

Good Health Should Be a Goal

Our aim is not simply to appreciate the gift of life, but to *care* for ourselves and our health. The number of years we live is not as important as the quality of life. This quality includes the period of time we experience an active, exciting and productive lifestyle. There are no guarantees, but one way to put the odds in our favor is to utilize healthy eating habits and regular exercise. Like anything worthwhile in life, it is not always easy or convenient. However, it offers the short-term benefit of increased alertness, energy and weight control. In the long-term, it may even extend your life. I encourage you to make it a regular part of your life.

Personal leadership includes the desire to care for and nurture this incredibly designed body we have been given. We need to discipline ourselves to maintain and maximize the health we presently have. We can only get the most out of life when we "feel good" and are not distracted by illness or pain. Some of the statistics and suggestions I will now provide in this chapter are gleaned from the January 2006 issue of *Consumer Reports* magazine published in the United States by Consumers Union.

Our culture has even built in an economic incentive to remain *inactive* in the workplace. Most work places have been designed for us to remain inactive since it is considered "inefficient" when people leave their desks. Yet, the human body was designed to be *active* and physical, not frozen in a static position looking at computer screens or talking on the telephone. To compensate for this lack of activity and to remain physically fit, it is important for us to exercise *regularly*.

Personal Recommendation

What do I personally recommend? I am an avid believer in walking *briskly* either outside or on a treadmill. Again, please remember to get your doctor's approval before you start *any* intense exercise program, and be sure to start slowly. It is best to *gradually* increase the length or intensity of your exercise routine. Walking is natural and has many benefits. It does not require any special equipment unless we desire to walk on a treadmill for convenience. It requires no special clothes except for a good quality pair of walking shoes. You are not required to learn any special skills, and if done outside, the view is constantly changing. Recent studies show that a thirty minute walk at 2.5 miles per hour will burn 173 calories for a two hundred pound person. Walking benefits your cardiovascular, weight-bearing and lower body fitness development. According to William Haskell, Ph.D., professor of medicine at Stanford University, "There are good, solid studies showing that sedentary adults who take up walking have significant improvements in risk factors associated with chronic disease." Look for ways to increase your opportunity to walk. For example, park your car farther back in the parking lot and enjoy a longer walk. Rather than take an elevator to travel a few floors up, why not walk the stairs?

The only exercises you should need to supplement walking briskly is *resistance* (push or pull against weight) and *upper body* strengthening, which is typically achieved by lifting free weights. Free weights are barbells, dumbbells, and kettlebells. Unlike weight machines, they do not limit you to specific, fixed movements. We are not talking about the lifting of heavy weights to build bulk. Free weights of five or ten pound "dumbbells" are all that is needed. According to the consumer magazine I mentioned earlier, between the ages of twenty and fifty a healthy adult has basically a fixed amount of muscle mass. After age fifty it begins to erode if we don't *resistance-train* with weights. By age eighty, sedentary adults have only about *sixty percent* of the muscle mass they had as active young adults. Building muscle mass also helps us to consume more calories to simply sustain the existing muscle. Your body consumes an extra thirty-five to fifty calories a day for every pound of muscle you add to your body.

The benefits of resistance training are also very functional to the human body, such as being able to push yourself out of a chair or walk up stairs without your legs hurting. Dr. William J. Kraemer, Ph.D., professor of kinesiology at the University of Connecticut has stated, "What puts the majority of people in convalescent homes is their inability to use their *hip flexor muscles* to get out of a chair or off the toilet." Weight training can also slow down the loss of bone mass in our bodies keeping our bones stronger. Finally, exercising with free weights can also help us to maintain our sense of steadiness and balance. Losing our balance and becoming physically unsteady also tends to increase with age.

Combining intense walking five days a week with a balanced weight routine to be completed three days a week can help a person become more active, more alert during the day, and proactive about health. The experts now believe we need to exercise about *150 minutes per week* at a level that is moderately intense to maintain our weight and tone our bodies. If you want to lose weight, you may need to workout up to *300 minutes per week* along with consuming a healthy, balanced diet. If you are not presently walking, please get into some alternative type of consistent and regular cardiovascular regimen. I encourage you to do something you enjoy. If it is fun, you are more likely to stick with it and perform it more consistently. Another tip is to choose the same time of day for exercising that is most convenient to you and your busy lifestyle. As the modern marketing slogan reminds us, "Just do it."

What We Eat is Important

Have you ever heard the saying, "You are what you eat?" There is a lot of truth to this statement, beginning with how much we eat. Americans are now more obese than ever before, and we have the associated chronic diseases to prove it. From 1976 to the year 2000, obesity in the United States increased from 14.4 percent to 30.9 percent of the population. Among the American populace, 34 percent of adult women are considered obese and 28 percent of men. Obesity can produce some debilitating chronic illnesses with an *increased* risk of diabetes, stroke, heart disease, breast cancer, hypertension, arthritis and gallstones. According to the *Centers for Disease Control and Prevention,* women take in an average of 335 *more* calories per day than they did thirty years ago, men take in 168 *more* calories than they did thirty years ago.

Part of the problem is in the *size* of the portions we eat. In our fast food "super-size it" world, more food is marketed to us as being somehow better. This simply is not true, and eating too much is unhealthy. Excess food consumption provides more calories than our bodies need to perform well. These excess calories are turned into fat by our body, and this leads to obesity. In 1957, a typical "fast food" burger weighed about an ounce. By 1997, the typical burger grew to six ounces, and now one-half pound burgers are marketed as normal and supposedly desirable. In the year 2002, the average American consumed *137 pounds* of beef, chicken, fish and shellfish. We also eat outside the home more than ever. In 1997, about 46 percent of a family's average food expenditures were for meals purchased outside the home, and 34 percent of these expenditures were for *fast foods.*

I travel quite a bit around the United States, and a typical restaurant meal also has food portions that are far too large. On top of this, the server will be sure to remind you to save room for a large dessert. It took me many years to overcome a problem I developed as a child. I was taught to eat *everything* set before me on my plate. I was reminded that all food was precious and limited because there were "starving children in China." This inbred sense of guilt I developed as a child was carried with me for many years. Whenever I ate out at a restaurant, I felt obligated to eat everything the chef had put on the plate. I felt bloated if I ate everything on my plate but guilty (wasteful) if I left food on it. I simply had to retrain my mind to only eat until moderately full and leave the rest behind.

What about the types of food we eat? This also requires dietary balance and a proactive approach in order to achieve a healthy lifestyle. A healthy diet should ideally consist of lots of whole grains, green vegetables, fruits, and nuts. Secondarily, it should include moderate portions of meat, fish, and dairy products. Our goal should be to replace the amount of simple carbohydrates we consume, with *complex* carbohydrates and proteins.

What We Drink is Important

Here is a riddle for you. What is 75 percent of the human body composed of, and what also comprises 85 percent of the human brain? It is also one *major* substance most of us don't get enough of. If you answered water, you are right. The need for water is just now being more deeply understood by the medical community, and here is a major reason why we need a lot of it. Our bodies have a built in detoxification system called our *lymphatic system*. It is a pathway of lymph nodes and small ducts that recirculate fluids from our tissues back to the heart and kidneys. One of its roles is to eliminate toxins from our body. We need lots of water to facilitate and improve the flow of the lymphatic system to purge our body of toxins. One way this flow can be stimulated naturally is through exercise, especially swimming and bouncing on a mini-trampoline. Another natural way is to drink plenty of fresh water to aid in the recirculation process of the system.

Water is the main solvent for all minerals, vitamins and food that are eventually assimilated into the body. It transports into the body needed sustenance and transports out of the body toxic substances so they can be eliminated. There is good reason why our blood is about 94 percent water when we are fully hydrated. Unfortunately, we live in a culture where marketers tell us that sugary and caffeinated beverages are preferred over plain water because they taste good or give us a "buzz." We can maximize our health by consuming more clean filtered water in the course of a day. Try to drink water that is not tainted with potentially toxic chemicals like chlorine, fluoride, pesticides or dangerous bacteria. Chlorine can be removed by simply exposing the water to air in an open container for half an hour. However, other pollutants are not so easy to eliminate. For this reason, a good activated carbon filter or other purification method may be a sound investment in your home.

From DNA to PMA

As noted earlier, our DNA is a great determining factor of who and what we are in a physical way through our genetic code. But there is another side of life with which we also need to be concerned and interested. I believe that just as much as our DNA, it also affects who and what we are. I call it our PMA, or positive mental attitude. This is obviously not a technical medical term, but it succinctly describes *how* we think, including our attitudes and how we each view the world around us. Having a right PMA energizes our emotional and mental health. Previously, we discussed maintaining and improving our physical health to maximize our personal leadership. Now we need to spend some more time on understanding our emotional and mental heath and how we can improve it.

To achieve great things as a personal leader requires a *positive* vision. It mentally pictures the future as better and more enriching than the world is today. It is this vision that motivates the leader during difficult and challenging times. But if our minds are constantly filled with self-doubt or negativity, we will soon *lose* our vision of a better tomorrow. An ancient Hebrew philosopher once wrote, "As a face is reflected in water, so a person is reflected by his heart." What we really are on the inside is reflected by how we see ourselves and react toward others. If you want to make your life or this world a better place, you must develop and maintain a positive PMA.

In reality, your life is going to follow your thoughts. If your thoughts are negative, they will draw in more negative thoughts. In life we tend to get exactly what we expect. If we live in the past, or if we have failed a number of times in the past, we may incorrectly *label* ourselves as failures. If this is the case, we must reprogram our thinking to get rid of this limiting and self-defeating mindset. A pessimistic attitude generates more stress, aggravation and personal discouragement because it expects and believes the worst of most situations. Some doctors now believe up to *ninety percent* of all medical diseases may be caused by internal stress and anxiety. The truth is that a negative attitude can have a detrimental impact on our health.

Historical Example of the Benefit of PMA

I would like to give you an example of a man who maintained a positive mental attitude (PMA) in spite of a string of great personal trials and tragedy. What he personally experienced would have broken anyone who lacked PMA. Thomas Jefferson left a legacy of being a remarkable and accomplished man. He is known as the third President of the United States and author of the American Declaration of Independence. Less known are his other lifetime achievements, including Virginia State Governor, American Vice President, Secretary of State, American Minister to France, architect, inventor, philosopher and founder of the University of Virginia. Yet, one particular *decade* of his life that brought about tremendous personal achievement also provided a number of serious personal tragedies.

In 1773, Jefferson's father-in-law died. Shortly afterward his best childhood friend died suddenly, leaving a wife and six children. The next year his first daughter Jane was born, but she would die eighteen months later when Jefferson was thirty one years old. In 1776, his mother died unexpectedly when she was only fifty seven. One year later, Jefferson's first son was born and died within a few hours of birth.

In 1781, a continuing *series* of personal trials occurred. First, the British army invaded Virginia and captured his beloved home Monticello. Jefferson barely escaped capture by the army. He broke his left wrist while being thrown from a horse. Also during this year, his reputation was damaged when his political enemies convinced the Virginia State Assembly to investigate his conduct as governor of Virginia. The very next year, his wife Martha died just a few months after giving birth to their daughter Lucy Elizabeth. On her deathbed, she made him promise never to marry again. Jefferson was now only thirty-nine years old, and he kept his promise to Martha. Though he would live another forty-three years, he never did marry again.

Most of us would certainly agree that Thomas Jefferson experienced many distressing personal trials during this ten to twelve year period. But, sad to say, that was not all. At the age of forty-one, he witnessed the death of his daughter Lucy Elizabeth, who died of "whooping cough." One year later, he stumbled while walking and broke his right wrist. It was not set properly, and he suffered pain in this wrist for the rest of his life. During various times of his life, he also suffered from prolonged migraine headaches that almost incapacitated him. Another worry he experienced was mounting debt for allowing his farm to deteriorate while he served his country in various roles.

All these events were happening while Jefferson was involved in the leadership of founding and managing a fragile new nation. History has recorded all of his many achievements during the very years these personal trials occurred in his life. Yet, few understand what was going on in his private life. He suffered more distressing personal trials than most of us have. However, Jefferson is not remembered for his many trials, but for his *accomplishments* as a powerful and effective leader.

Jefferson had one great leadership quality that set him apart from many others. He did not allow the difficult circumstances of life to crush his *inner spirit* or his desire to serve others who called upon him for help. Yes, like all of us, he could become very discouraged. Upon the death of his wife, he remarked to others that he even wanted to end his own life, and he entered a period of severe grief. Yes, he certainly hurt, mourned, and experienced depression and sadness like most of us. Yet he was able to reach *deep* inside, rise above these natural emotions and go forward. Even with these great personal tragedies, he attempted to stay in a positive frame of mind. Thomas Jefferson was able to endure great personal hardship in life because he was a man of purpose. He viewed the purpose of life itself as an opportunity to explore knowledge and change the world around him. Many of the political freedoms we enjoy today are a result of the PMA he maintained during some very difficult times in his personal life. Maintaining a *positive attitude* toward life is so important; we will discuss this in greater detail in Principle #11.

It's an Inside Job

We produce what we continually put in front of us. If it is negative, the end result will be unconstructive. If it is positive, the end result will be productive and of great value. You cannot give birth to something you did not first conceive and envision. That means we must keep in front of us what we want to achieve. How do we keep a positive vision in front of us? Paint a picture of your vision on the canvas of your heart. Allow it to motivate and inspire you through good times and bad. It must become part of your belief and value system. It must start *deeply* on the inside before it will ever happen on the outside. Don't paint it on doubt, fear or limited thinking. You will never rise any higher than your mental attitude and image allows. You will never accomplish things you can't imagine yourself accomplishing.

Again, the first mistake many individuals make is that they are limited by their vision and have painted a negative picture of themselves in their hearts. Be aware that much of the so-called "entertainment industry" in the world today is negative and destructive to a PMA. Much of our news, music, films and television accentuate the negative.

To be an effective personal leader, you must have an optimistic approach toward life and toward others. Raise your level of expectancy about life, and good things will begin to happen. Again, we must believe the best on the inside before it can happen on the outside. We must consciously choose to live with an attitude that good things are going to happen every day. It is a psychological principle that we move *toward* what we see in ourselves or others. If we see ourselves as making positive personal changes and helping others to grow, we will have a strong, healthy self-image. Our self-image is a portrait of who and what we picture ourselves to be in the world around us.

If you have been plagued by a negative image of yourself or of others, it is time to *reprogram* your attitude and thinking. We don't always get what we deserve in life, but we usually get what we expect. In the long run we receive what we believe. If we expect mediocrity, that is exactly what we will achieve because we become what we expect and believe. It is time to change what you expect and to stop living with negatively limiting thoughts. Start by understanding this clear principle: "I am what I am today because of what I believed about myself yesterday. I will become tomorrow what I believe about myself right now."

Watch Your Self-talk

Take an *inventory* of your personal thoughts and self-talk. Self-talk is the constant communication you have with yourself when you are conscious. How healthy is this important dialogue? Do you find it to be basically positive, optimistic and productive, or is it negative and highly critical of most things? What we have programmed into our minds determines how we are going to function on a daily basis. If we go through the day never expecting anything good to happen and feeling unworthy, we will make this belief a *self*-fulfilling prophecy. When a negative thought arrives, make a conscious decision to replace it with a positive thought. Make an effort to "catch" yourself doing this. Ask your loved ones to point out to you when you are speaking or acting in a negative way. Start reading, listening to and absorbing positive communication that promotes productive ideas. Associate with folks who have a lifestyle that demonstrates a healthy PMA. Don't become discouraged if you find yourself slipping back into critical habits or attitudes. After all, it took you many years to develop this *chronic* nature, and it will take some time to overcome it.

The beautiful premise behind every new day is that it holds the promise of a fresh start. It provides the opportunity to do something different, start something new, break a bad habit, or establish a good habit. In other words, it gives us the power to choose a new course or direction in life. So why don't we typically appreciate or acknowledge this fact? Why do we continue to "choose" to do the same old things every day, including some that are detrimental to us? The answer lies in our lifestyle and mind-set. We are culturally programmed to desire comfort and resist change. We often *know* we should change things, and we promise ourselves we will do it someday. The problem is that "someday" never seems to come, and eventually we all run out of *somedays*. This self-imposed "comfort zone" convinces us that change is always something we can do tomorrow. But here is an absolute truth: Today is a gift, and tomorrow is promised to no one.

Recap of Principle #3

All of us have different personality orientations. Those with a strong internal locus of control tend to believe that their lives and events can be influenced by their own actions and choices. Those with a strong external locus of control tend to believe that chance or fate is the deciding factor in life and that their actions have little influence. This can also affect how we view the importance of maintaining our health. To maximize our health, we need to exercise regularly and eat healthy foods. Avoid the tendency to use various common excuses to evade the need for exercise. A good exercise program includes a combination of cardiovascular conditioning and resistance training.

To achieve a better tomorrow, we must get a *new* vision and change the image we have within us today. Don't simply focus on where you are now, but also focus on where you want to be. It may take a large amount of personal growth, self-sacrifice and maturity to get to your destination, but the time to start is right now. Remember, you will become what you keep in front of you. Develop and maintain a positive mental attitude (PMA). You can *repaint* your vision on the canvas of your heart. Learn to focus on what you can do and on the possibilities. Start expecting things to change for the better, and see yourself in a fresh new way. If you do this, you will not only have a powerful impact on your own life, but also a positive influence on the lives of others.

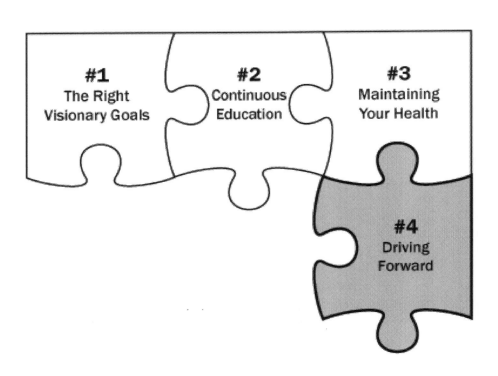

PRINCIPLE #4

DRIVING FORWARD

One of the classic dictionary definitions of the word *drive* is "to supply the emotional or physical energy that leads somebody to act or behave in an extreme way." This is an important principle of personal leadership. Servant-leaders are not content with the status quo; they are always looking for ways to improve themselves and the world around them. Whereas most people are content with the way they are, or the way our present world is structured, genuine leaders are motivated by a better vision of the future. Personal leadership demands that this better future start within the self. It is this inner vision that generates the *drive* needed to achieve great things. It is our personal vision that fuels drive, and without that vision we will quickly run out of gas and lose our enthusiasm.

Earlier I mentioned how I was not motivated to be a good student, and I did not perform well. Coming from a "blue-collar" background, I was also not encouraged to attend college. My high school classes were all centered around becoming an electrician. My classes were tailored more toward the vocational training I would need to begin a career as a construction worker. But then something changed inside me.

In my senior year, I decided that I wanted to go to college to get an undergraduate degree. But I didn't want to go to just any college. I wanted to attend a small private college located in Pasadena, California. I knew I could get the personalized attention and training there that I needed to have a well-rounded liberal arts education. They had the reputation of accepting approximately five out of every one-hundred applications, but I confidently applied anyway. The letter I received back was devastating. Not only was my application denied, but the Registrar told me not to bother applying again because I was "not the kind of quality" they were looking for.

From that day on, my major goal in life was to attend that college. I was rejected again the next year (in 1972), but I considered it a minor setback. For the next four years, until I was accepted as a student in 1976, I learned a lot about the meaning of the word "drive" and the power behind it.

Analogy of an Automobile

We can expand our understanding of this principle by examining how an automobile is *driven*. An automobile is a machine that has an internal engine pushing the vehicle in a certain direction. We call this driving the automobile, and it responds by going in the direction we steer it toward. Often when we are driving toward a desired destination, a number of obstacles are encountered. For example, if we drive a car uphill or against the wind, there is greater resistance against the momentum of the vehicle. This is also true when we drive in the rain or on snowy roads. When this occurs, we are able to take steps to signal to the engine that greater energy is required to overcome the added resistance against the automobile. Inside the engine is the power to generate the right *resources* at the right time to continue on our journey. The automobile is designed to respond and provide extra horsepower to overcome natural obstacles. The same can be said of the drive required to achieve the goals and vision we desire.

Much like an automobile that has an internal engine, we have been created with the human mind that has incredible untapped resources. Scientists are just now beginning to understand the enormous creative potential that exists within each person. It is our passion, inspired by a clear personal vision that will impel us to move *forward* through obstacles. The greatest enemy of achievement is a half-hearted effort, and this is always caused by an inability to push ourselves when we face resistance. It is our own drive that will propel us toward our goals even when all the odds seem to be against us. It is also our determination and example of relentless drive that will inspire others to join us in a worthy cause. Drive is contagious, and seeing people who have this quality motivates others to want to be part of something bigger than themselves. If you seem to lack the drive needed to prod yourself to achieve the things you desire, it is because you do not have a clear *inner* vision of a desired future. Similar to the way an athlete prepares for an event by "envisioning" the perfect performance, our vision must become real to us. We must get excited about it and picture it so vividly that we can imagine how achieving it will feel, taste, smell and look. This is the kind of vision that prods us to move mountains if necessary to get important things accomplished. Possessing a clear vision generates drive, and it is this characteristic called "drive" that never permits us to give up and quit.

Example of William Wilberforce

The tenacious William Wilberforce was a philanthropist, British politician and leader who worked tirelessly to abolish slavery in the British Empire. At the age of twenty-one and while still a student, Wilberforce was first elected as a Member of Parliament (MP). Due to a wealthy inheritance, he drifted through life enjoying all the social benefits that money could buy. But, through a gradual religious awakening and the influence of friends, he came to believe that slavery was repugnant and immoral. As a politician, he knew that the abolition of slavery could only be achieved in stages and that there would be great political resistance during every step. His first goal was to get Parliament to pass a law outlawing the *transporting* of slaves on British ships. Secondly, only after this was achieved, the full emancipation of slaves could eventually be accomplished by law. Even though he was rather small and sickly with poor eyesight and chronic gastrointestinal problems, he was blessed with a gifted voice and dynamic eloquence. He often used this skill in Parliament to persuade others. Author James Boswell witnessed one of his political speeches and remarked, "I saw what seemed a mere shrimp mount upon the table; but as I listened, he grew, and grew, until the shrimp became a whale."

In April of 1791, Wilberforce introduced a parliamentary bill to abolish the slave trade during a four-hour speech. However, the nation was not ready for what appeared to be a radical social position. Many years passed, and a war with France, along with changing political parties and prime ministers, delayed the passage of the bill. It was not until March 1807—about 16 *years* later—that Wilberforce, driven by his beliefs and deeply held values, achieved his goal.

In declining health he passionately continued his involvement in the anti-slavery movement even after he resigned from Parliament. Wilberforce died three days after hearing that the passage of the *Slavery Abolition Act* was assured in July of 1833. For over forty-two years his drive pushed him onward to finally reach his goal of the total emancipation of slaves in the British Empire. It is estimated that nearly 800,000 slaves were freed due to his relentless efforts.

Example of Thomas Edison

Another example of a man with a tremendous drive was the famous inventor Thomas Alva Edison. In his lifetime he achieved an unbelievable

1093 U.S. patents. There were many other fine inventors in the late nineteenth century and early twentieth century like Elihu Thomson, Nikola Tesla, Elisha Gray, Edward Weston and George Phelps. However, what set Edison apart from others was his clear vision of a better world. He envisioned a concept we now call "innovation" that included invention, research, development and commercialization. While others were content to simply invent and seek patents, Edison knew that the continued development and commercialization of discoveries were necessary to truly change the world for the better. His unquenchable drive is responsible for the invention of the phonograph, motion-picture camera and practical improvements that made the telegraph, telephone and incandescent light bulb a reality. His vision created entire industries, including electric utilities and the film and recording industries.

We will now focus on just the drive that Edison demonstrated in his improvement of the electric light bulb. In 1811, Sir Humphry Davy discovered that when an electric arc was passed between two poles, light was produced. By 1841, experimental arc lights were installed in Paris, but they burned out too quickly. It was theorized that if the right conductor or filament was discovered and it was electrified in a container without oxygen, it might be possible to create a practical electric light. Sir Joseph Wilson Swan was the first to construct an electric light bulb, but he had a problem maintaining a vacuum in the bulb and it burned out too quickly. About the same time Swan was working on his invention, Edison was also working on a similar project. What Edison achieved is the product of a clear vision that *motivated* his unwavering drive to make something happen. From 1878 to 1880, Edison and his associates worked on over 3000 different theories to develop an efficient and marketable light bulb. The key would be in discovering a useful filament, and what Edison did achieve is a tribute to persistence and drive.

In 1876, Edison opened the first laboratory dedicated to industrial research in Menlo Park, New Jersey. Because of Swan's experiments, Edison became convinced that carbonizing materials would lead to the right kind of filament. He tested the fibers of virtually every known vegetative plant in the world. The "Wizard of Menlo Park" even contacted biologists and asked them to send him rare plant fibers from the tropics. He would conduct so many experiments that he maintained his own glass blowing shed where the fragile glass bulbs were crafted for his constant experiments. He later wrote, "Before I got through I tested no fewer than 6,000 vegetable growths, and ransacked the world for the most suitable filament material." Most people would have given up at ten experiments, or one hundred or one thousand, but Edison would not be defeated. Eventually, he used a carbonized cotton thread filament, and it produced a soft orange glow for fifteen hours. By 1880, he had developed a 16-watt bulb that lasted 1500 hours, and a usable light bulb was ready to be produced and commercialized. His unrelenting drive paid off, and he forever changed the modern world. His personal example of drive and commitment inspired those who worked with him.

It is obvious that Edison had a large amount of personal drive, but he was not single-minded or incapable of multitasking. He did not work on just one project and become oblivious to everything else around him. He had the ability to work on several *different* projects at the same time.

You may be saying to yourself that this is certainly an impressive example of personal drive. Yes, Edison could prod himself to achieve great things. But you may be saying to yourself, look at all the excellent resources he had. The rest of us don't have laboratories in which to perform experiments. We don't have teams of workers to help us make our dreams come true. Most of us don't have financial backers or investors to help us fund our visions of a better future. Yes, there is no doubt that at this point in Edison's life, he had acquired many resources to bring innovation to the world. However, don't lose sight of my major point.

All the resources in the world won't compensate for a *lack* of drive. On the other hand, with a large amount of drive and little else, great personal visions and goals can come to fruition. Now I would like to relate to you an example I have personally witnessed in my own lifetime.

A Modern Example

In the middle of the 1970s, I had an opportunity to attend a small private college in Pasadena, California. I attained my undergraduate degree at this institution. Like most colleges in America, it was founded by a religious leader who had a clear, specific vision of what he wanted to achieve within his own mind. His name was Herbert W. Armstrong. With an advertising background, he had previously experienced a number of business failures during the "Great Depression." With his knowledge of advertising, he wanted to create a news-oriented magazine that would appeal to a vast audience. Its articles would analyze *world news* events and be blended with a subtle religious message. He envisioned it as an international magazine with potentially millions of subscribers.

In 1927, Armstrong made a "mockup" of the magazine he envisioned. Yet there were many obstacles that got in his way, including a lack of finances and other limited resources. For about seven years he was unable to continue his dream, and virtually nothing progressed with the magazine. I am sure that other priorities and many other distractions arose to obstruct his goal. For most people, this would have been the end of their dream of a new magazine. Most would have allowed the idea to "die on the vine." But he never gave up on his vision, and Armstrong prodded himself to slowly but surely continue the project. It was not until February of 1934 that he published the *first* issue of the magazine. He published about 250 copies by hand on a mimeograph machine and was both the editor and author of most articles. Yet again, other roadblocks arose, and he was unable to publish the magazine regularly. By the middle of 1935, Armstrong had ceased its regular publication. He had virtually no financial resources, no associates to help him write or edit articles, and obstacles in every other direction. What this man did have was an unrelenting drive and a vision. By now most folks would have given up on their dream and moved on to other things. Many would say to themselves at this juncture that "I tried and it just didn't work out," and they might give up satisfied that they did their best. But, this religious leader (who was by now making regular radio broadcasts) was not a quitter. He had the drive to see his vision come to completion even if he would be forced to delay this heartfelt goal due to numerous challenges and circumstances. He drove himself and never forgot about his vision of the new magazine he named *The Plain Truth*, named after Benjamin Franklin's famous pamphlet printed in 1747.

It was not until January of 1938 (two and one-half years after it had temporarily ceased publication) that he began printing the magazine once again. It was now *eleven years* since he had originally conceived the concept of this publication. Once again, it was a hand produced mimeographed magazine with only 1050 subscribers on its mailing list. Over the next few years, the future of the magazine was in question due to continuing challenges with finances. Eventually the magazine was regularly published on a monthly basis, and it grew steadily in subscribers from the 1940s through the 1980s. Over the years it expanded from being an eight-page black and white mimeographed publication to a thirty-six page full color publication. By the time of Armstrong's death in 1986, the magazine had over six million subscribers and was published in seven languages. It was estimated that up to *twenty million* readers worldwide read the magazine each month, and it was published by one of the largest printing houses in the United States.

Numerous times this vision of a biblically-oriented news magazine faced near extinction, but it was the *drive* of one man who prodded himself and others around him to overcome substantial obstacles to turn a dream into a major and influential magazine. Herbert Armstrong's theology may have been controversial and nontraditional, but it is hard to argue with what he accomplished through his personal drive.

My Own Experience

What you are holding in your hands is one of my dreams. It was originally conceived in 1992 with all of the twelve principles that appear in this book. A close friend of mine joined me in incorporating a business, and we hoped to publish much of what appears in this publication. But, we had very limited finances. At the time we were both raising young families and could only pool together a small amount of money. We spent some money advertising, but it was soon gone. We made a sample cassette tape to promote the first principle. We even printed some brochures to promote the principles, but with few financial resources left, we eventually had to dissolve the business. But the dream was not forgotten. Twelve years later, in February of 2004, I wrote and published the *introduction* to the twelve principles in weLEAD Online Magazine. Each principle appeared one at a time over the next four years. The moral of the story is this: a dream delayed but not forgotten can still be a dream fulfilled.

In July 2008, Dr. Randy Pausch died from pancreatic cancer at age forty-seven. He became an instant celebrity when his 76-minute last lecture entitled "Really Achieving Your Childhood Dreams" became an Internet sensation. Pausch talked about what his childhood dreams taught him about life. He also co-wrote a book, *The Last Lecture,* which became a best-seller. Pausch wrote:

> The brick walls are there for a reason. The brick walls are not there
> to keep us out; the brick walls are there to give us a chance to show
> how badly we want something. The brick walls are there to stop
> the people who don't want it badly enough.

How badly we really want to achieve something is demonstrated by our amount of drive and determination to reach our goals.

Recap of Principle #4

The ability to push yourself during difficult or stressful times is an *essential* principle for personal leadership. You may have established the right visionary goal (Principle #1), you may have invested well in the education needed to excel in your chosen field (Principle #2), and you may be living a positive lifestyle that enhances your health and personal well-being (Principle #3). That is wonderful, but if you lack the drive needed to *prod* yourself toward a vision, you will stall out when you face stiff resistance or roadblocks placed in your path. If you don't believe in your own vision and show others how excited you are to achieve it, why will they want to join you?

Much like the analogy of a vehicle we discussed earlier, there will be times when you have to use more energy to prevail against added resistance. You will need to reach deep down inside yourself to tap into additional resources like passion, persistence, and even plain stubbornness. Fire yourself up by thinking about what a better future will be like for others and yourself. If you don't passionately believe in your *own* dreams, who else will?

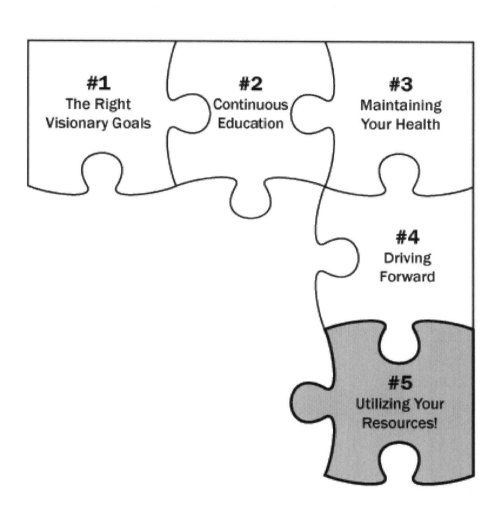

PRINCIPLE #5

UTILIZING YOUR RESOURCES

Have you heard the story about a truck that got stuck under a bridge? It is said that a box truck was attempting to pass under a large bridge. As the truck driver approached the structure, he felt there was enough room to clear the bottom of the steel and concrete deck of the bridge. But as he was passing under, he suddenly heard a loud screeching noise! The screech turned into a grind, and the lurching truck came to a dead stop. It was now wedged under the bridge and could go neither forward nor backward. Traffic came to a complete standstill, and naturally the local authorities were called out to examine the situation. How would they get the truck out from under the bridge?

From the Mouth of Babes

A tow truck was sent out to try to pull the vehicle free. A county engineer arrived to examine this difficult situation. There were deep discussions and many measurements were made. Various calculations were performed to determine how much of the truck or bridge would be destroyed if the vehicle was simply yanked or pulled out. If too much of the bridge's concrete was broken in the process, it might cause the bridge to become unsafe. What if road equipment was brought in to dig beneath the vehicle tires to lower it? What if heavy equipment was brought in to lift the bridge just a few inches? Traffic continued to back up, and discussions raged on as frustrated workers and authorities pondered this difficult problem. A crowd also gathered around the scene to watch all the exciting activity and hubbub. A worker was walking by part of the crowd and surveying the situation, when a little boy who had previously been riding his bicycle and had stopped to glare, said to the man, "Why not let some of the *air* out of the tires?"

"What?" asked the worker in incredulous shock. "What did you say?"

The boy repeated, "Why not let the air out of the tires?" From this *simple* observation and statement, an easy and effective solution was found to a difficult problem that had confounded some very bright and energetic people.

What the little boy demonstrated is what every effective personal leader needs to achieve success. The boy had imagination and was tapping into his mental resources. Within his mind, he dug deep for a *creative* solution and envisioned the vehicle dropping down because the tires would lower the vehicle when air was removed from them. It was this imagination that gave the boy the resourcefulness to solve a serious problem. Sadly, most researchers tell us that we lose a part of our creativity as we age. The innovative skills we learn at *play* as children become lost as we enter adulthood. However, many solutions to difficult problems are easily solved if we learn to use our imagination and mentally step outside our comfort zones. This is a common problem in business today. Many managers believe that it takes millions of dollars and a severe culture shock to solve large problems in their organizations. As mentioned in the example above, when mountains are made out of molehills, problem-solving can become more difficult and costly than it really needs to be.

Analytical Thinking May Not Be Enough

As a leader, there will be many times when emergencies, unexpected circumstances or complications arise to block the path to your goals. There will also be times when rational and analytical thinking isn't good enough to make the right or best decision. This is where we need to use our *ingenuity* as a resource to remove or to go around any obstacles. Tapping into our resources will require mental agility, physical capacity, or knowing where to go for help.

During these kinds of demanding situations, we should never panic. We need clear heads and calm emotions to think logically and rapidly. In addition, we *also* need to maintain composure for our imaginations to be most effective and in order to help us arrive at wise decisions.

Earlier, we spoke about the essential need for vision. It is a compelling vision that feeds our desire to accomplish great things in life. Remember that our personal visions are the mental pictures we have that inspire us to seek out our goals during good times and bad. In this principle we will discuss the ability to tap into our imaginations to solve the problems that threaten to block us from achieving our goals. Once we arrive at an answer, we need to do something with it. This can be especially difficult for leaders who have a "black or white" view of the world. If we define every person, event or activity as "good or bad" or "right or wrong," we greatly limit our ability to solve problems creatively. The truth is that some things are indeed "good or bad," but most things are neutral unless they are misused. Having a healthy, creative imagination to solve problems requires us to be *open*-minded and to look for the good in others or events, not the worst.

The Power of Imagination

Obviously, solving a problem requires that we keep going forward without quitting. Imagination is the resource that even helps us to plow through an obstacle when necessary. Some folks have a vivid imagination naturally and have reputations as "idea people." But most of us need to do some research, seek advice and perform some analysis to "prime the pump" of our powers of invention. It often requires us to think differently than we normally do. Asking a series of "what if . . ." questions can often spark innovative solutions. Organizations have found that the creativity generated during "brainstorming" sessions can be very productive. However, the potential solutions we ponder should *always* be legal, ethical and not harmful to others. Sadly, our prisons are populated with some very creative and imaginative individuals. But they allowed their ingenuity to be used selfishly and to harm other people.

It is also important to realize that there is usually more than one solution to most problems. Even though it is desirable to find the best solution, it is not always practical. When this occurs, be open-minded, and don't delay making a critical decision because you are searching for the perfect answer. Some managers even use this as an excuse not to make the important decisions that *need* to be made. When you have faced a difficult challenge and used your imagination as a resource to discover a solution, don't stop there.

It is not enough to have imagination as a resource if you are unwilling to make the hard decisions. Possessing the right answer without the strength or will to implement it will not solve difficult problems. Some folks are good at finding solutions but struggle to make decisions.

Story of the Bible Salesman

A young man wanted to sell Bibles for a living going from house to house in his local community. Unfortunately, he had struggled with a "stuttering" speech impediment since birth. The first week was very discouraging, and he was called into the office of the sales manager to report on how his first week went. The young man was intimidated by the stern appearance of his manager. "How *many* Bibles did you *SELL* last week?" barked the sales manager.

The young man was unsettled and said, "I . . . I . . . I . . . so . . . so . . . sold . . . fi . . . fi . . . five . . . bi . . . bi . . . bi-bibles."

The sales manager quickly snapped, "You better SELL more than five next week, or you are fired!"

The next week the young man was again called into the office of the sales manager. Once again he heard the question, "How *many* Bibles did you *SELL* last week?"

The young man replied, "I . . . I . . . I . . . so . . . so . . . sold . . . fi . . . fi . . . *fifty* . . . bi . . . bi . . . bi-bibles."

The sales manager was shocked. "Fifty Bibles in one week is a record in our company. How in the world did you do it?"

The young man replied, "Well . . . I . . . I . . . I . . . sa . . . sa . . . said . . . to . . . to . . . the customers . . . do . . . do . . . do . . . you . . . you . . . you . . . wa . . . wa . . . want to bu . . . bu . . . bu . . . buy a bible or do . . . do . . . do . . . you want me to re . . . re . . . re . . . read . . . it to you?"

It is certainly not my intention to ridicule or degrade any person who has a speech impediment. But, there is an important moral to this humorous story. The young man utilized his personal *resources* to achieve his goal. Whatever personal qualities or traits we possess can be used as valuable resources even if we perceive them as negative characteristics.

Phyllis Diller was a thirty-eight year-old woman with five children, and they were living on welfare. At night she cleaned offices to earn some money to help pay the bills. One night she found a book in a trashcan entitled *The Magic of Believing* by Claude Bristol. That night she decided to read this book rather than clean the office, and it changed her life. The book gave her a valuable insight. It suggested that you take *your* greatest weakness and turn it into a personal strength. By looking in a mirror, Phyllis believed her greatest weakness was her looks. She felt she was downright ugly. She then proceeded to create comedy skits that focused on poking fun at her appearance and a fictional husband named "Fang."

In three years, she was working as a stand-up comedienne in Las Vegas shows, and she went on to have a long, successful career. Phyllis Diller is now considered to be one of the pioneers of female stand-up comedy. Like the Bible salesman, she utilized her personal resources to achieve her goals. In her case, it was by turning her greatest weakness into a *new* strength. (By the way, she is also an accomplished pianist as well as a painter.)

From Greatest Weakness to a Strength

In 1976, I was finally accepted to the college I had dreamed about attending for many years. Rather than going to the campus in Pasadena, California, I chose to attend the sister campus in Big Sandy, Texas. When I arrived, I was soon to discover what real humiliation felt like. We were given a series of tests to see what kind of *additional* classes we needed to be successful at the college level. It was at this time that I fully realized how disadvantaged I was by attending a dreadful high school and not taking my classes more seriously.

My written English skills were so poor that I was put into a remedial class that was composed of me . . . and ten foreign students. None of them even had English as a first language, and a couple didn't even write English. Apparently, English was also my second language behind *Clevelandish*.

But, thanks to the loving attention of Mr. Heath, I worked hard to improve myself. I had a daily journal to write in, and many written assignments were required during this class. By the end of my freshman year, an article I wrote was published on the front page of the college newspaper. What you are now reading is the work of a man who decided, like the Bible salesman and Phyllis Diller, to turn his greatest weakness into a personal strength.

Making Decisions Can Be Risky

It is easy to understand why many leaders want to avoid making decisions. There are a number of valid reasons. First of all, it is often risky. Risk is defined as the possibility of suffering harm, loss or danger. We tend to be comfortable in our patterns and expectations. Oftentimes making a decision means we must step out of our "comfort zone" and into the unknown. Past experiences teach us that even a slight shift in our course can have dramatic effects on an outcome. On a personal level, we may determine the *right answers* but avoid making decisions about our families, careers or finances because of an aversion to risk and fear of failure.

Secondly, leaders often make decisions while they are slightly ahead of the prevailing group or culture. It is often a lonely, thankless experience with little visible support. This situation is often compounded *greatly* when the leader has not taken the time and energy to build a strong consensus among others.

But here is an important point about decision-making and risk: we will frequently come to a crossroad in life or business where an important decision must be made. Then we have a difficult choice to make. Either *we* make the decisions, or "time and chance" will decide for us what we were unwilling to decide for ourselves. Either way, a decision will be made. The question is, will we take charge and assume greater control of the outcome, or will we allow luck, chance or fate to determine the outcome for us?

There is an old story about two men drifting on a raft traveling down the Niagara River toward the ominous Niagara Falls. They began to argue about how far they were from the falls and when they should head the raft toward the shore. The argument continued and went on and on. While they bickered and delayed making a decision, time made the decision *for* them, with unfortunate results.

Wrong Decision or Indecision

I am not suggesting that you lurch into ill-advised or poor decision-making. This is especially true when making a long-term decision about a relationship like a marriage or becoming a parent. A bad relationship is poisonous, and has the potential to stifle all your hopes and dreams. For this kind of a decision, there is a clear right from wrong, and I recommend that you think long and hard before making a serious lifelong commitment.

However, the truth is that *most* of our daily life decisions are not as complicated as choosing a life partner. For these decisions a leader should seek the facts, get advice, do the research, and resourcefully find an answer.

But there does come a time when a decision—*the* decision--must be made. It has been said that former American President and World War II General Dwight D. Eisenhower once commented, "A wrong decision is better than indecision." Think about why a military general would have made this comment. A wrong decision is at least a choice, and if that choice is wrong, there is often enough time to retrench, regroup and alter the course. Creativity is flexible and can be modified early in the decision process. However, *indecision* only erodes precious time and often removes the option of an alternative choice from the decision-maker. Sometimes the real risk is not taking one. As author and educator Gary Dessler states, "Very few decisions are forever; there is more 'give' in most decisions than we realize. While many major strategic decisions are hard to reverse, most poor decisions won't mean the end of the world for you, so don't become frozen in the finality of your decision."

At the heart and core of leadership is also the willingness to take personal *responsibility* for a difficult decision. On June 6, 1944, during World War II,

General Eisenhower agonized over a difficult decision to allow Allied forces to land on the beaches of Normandy, France. The weather had been poor and threatened to derail the Allied assault. A window of opportunity was closing, and it was time for decisive action. Eisenhower finally gave approval for the landing. However, he also took the time to write an "official statement" to the media in case the landing failed and the Allies were unable to secure a beachhead. In his handwritten announcement, Eisenhower accepted full responsibility for the failure. Thankfully, it was never needed.

Programmed and Nonprogrammed Decisions

Many experts in management believe that not all decisions are the same. They differentiate between what they call *programmed* and *nonprogrammed* decisions. Programmed decisions are defined as ones that are repetitive and can typically be resolved through rational analysis and mechanical procedures. It is believed that the overwhelming majority of decisions we make are programmed decisions. Standard rules of logic and judgment can be applied to these decision types. Typically programmed decisions do not require a great degree of imagination.

On the other hand, *nonprogrammed* decisions are defined as unique in nature. These include *crisis* situations or arriving at personal *crossroads* in life. Nonprogrammed decisions rely *heavily* on our ethical values rather than clear-cut analysis. They are typically more urgent and require greater focus. We all must eventually face them: the tough, agonizing decisions that often need to be based on incomplete information and unknown criteria. Sometimes there is no clear choice of what or who is absolutely right or wrong. There may be little "black and white" to contrast, but rather a large shade of gray. Using our positive ethics and deep-seated values as a guide, we will need to muster all the creativity and intuition we can find deep within ourselves for good solutions. Because these nonprogrammed decisions are usually critical, the risk and consequences can be great, but don't let that stop you from taking action when required.

A Few Decision-Making Tips

After you have tapped into all of your available resources, here are a few *tips* to improve your decision-making ability.

Recognize the facts as they really are and not how you want to see them. It is easy to ignore or distort the truth because we already desire to support a particular answer. For example, those who study theology often fall prey to a problem called *proof-texting*. This is where the theologian first comes to a personal conviction and then *looks* for Scriptures to support a preconceived belief. Many scientists are also guilty of the same problem. Maintain your objectivity so your decision is based on an intelligent analysis of the actual facts and not a preconceived opinion.

Along with analysis, don't be afraid to use your heart as long as you are not blinded by raw emotion. A balanced decision is one that is made from both the head and the heart. This is where you make a decision based on accumulated experience, knowledge and intuition. Remember, having firm personal values and strong ethics is the *foundation* of good intuition. Psychiatrist Sigmund Freud stated:

> When making a decision of minor importance I have always found it advantageous to consider all the pros and cons. In vital matters, however, such as the choice of a mate or a profession, the decision should come from the unconscious, from somewhere within ourselves. In the important decisions of our personal life, we should be governed, I think, by the deep inner needs of our nature.

Obviously, if the "deep inner needs of our nature" are centered on integrity and genuine concern for others, our intuition will serve us well.

More Tips

Another decision-making tip is to be careful not to use shortcuts to save time. A common shortcut is called *heuristics*. This is used to speed up decision-making by applying "rules of thumb" to quickly reach a conclusion. For example, a senior manager may say, "I only want individuals with advanced degrees to apply for this position." Yes, this may speed up the selection process, but it may also mean the *best* qualified or most talented individual is not even considered for the position.

The final tip I offer is to avoid *anchoring*. The decision-making trait known as anchoring is where we give too much credence to the *first* communication or set of facts that we hear. This first bit of information then becomes the benchmark by which the decision will be made, and later information that is contrary to it is simply dismissed or minimized.

Recap of Principle #5

The next time you are confronted with the need to make a decision, remember the little boy gazing at the truck stuck under a bridge. The best answer will require using your imagination as a resource. Challenge yourself to think differently and from a fresh perspective. When you have made a decision and an answer is at hand, don't stop there. A leader's *calling* is to make the hard decisions when they are needed. No one said the job is easy. Yes, there is a risk to decision-making, but there is often a greater risk when we do nothing and allow fate to decide for us. So be sure you gather the facts, get sound advice, and do the necessary research. Look at all of the resources you have available to you including your imagination, financial options, educational background, and knowledgeable colleagues. Then utilize them to solve any problems or challenges you face.

Finally, go ahead and make the decision. If you get stuck . . . maybe you need to just step back and look at things differently. Perhaps you will even need to let some air out of the tires.

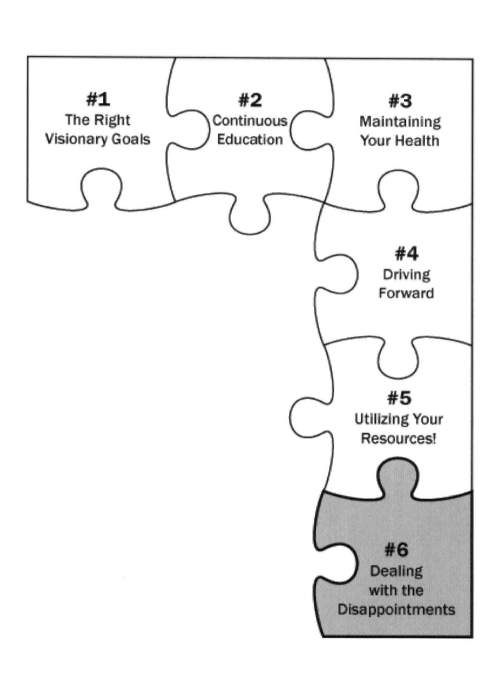

PRINCIPLE #6

DEALING WITH THE DISAPPOINTMENTS

We all come from different cultures and various backgrounds. The human race is very diverse. We are comprised of different colors, physical sizes, religious beliefs, political views, cultural backgrounds and local customs. However, as diverse as we are, there is a *universal* experience that personal leaders all have in common. It is the feeling of disappointment and discouragement. When we walk through the "valleys" of life, our daily activities seem to become a vicious circle. The cycle usually works something like this. A particular event occurs and we get discouraged, and it affects the qualities of our decision-making. We become frustrated, and stress takes a toll on our attitude. We become gloomy and begin to focus on the unfavorable aspect of every situation. The negative consequences of this perspective triggered under duress, gets us even more discouraged, and the cycle continues. The publication, *Leadership by the Book*, reminds us that "people who produce good results feel good about themselves." Unfortunately, the *reverse* is also true.

In my life there have been some deep disappointments. A few of the goals I have struggled so hard to achieve were major disappointments when I finally attained them. Some people and organizations I trusted were shallow, manipulative, and harmful. I know what it is like to *feel* disappointment and betrayal. I also know that I am not alone in these experiences, and that is why this principle is so important.

Most of the time, we may go through life at a seemingly even pace. Yes, we may have both good days and bad days, but they seem to balance themselves out as we proceed through life's journey. But then there are times when everything seems to go wrong. Decisions appear to be poor. We offend or hurt people we don't intend to harm. Our confidence seems to sag, and everything we "touch" seems to result in a negative outcome. We may begin to question our abilities or even lose sight of our personal goals or values. During this time, it is possible to *sink* into a period of melancholy and self-doubt regarding our past achievements or our vision of the future.

This is actually a common human trait. Every indication is that all the great (and not so great) leaders of human history have experienced periods of discouragement or mild depression. It is not the purpose of this book to discuss chronic clinical depression but the natural cycle of human discouragement which we all suffer from occasionally.

Examples of Discouragement

George Washington is remembered as the first president of the United States of America. However, before he held political office he was a military officer who was chosen by Congress to be general and commander-in-chief of the Continental Army. Washington wrote a stirring letter to the legislature of New Hampshire in December 1777. It was written during the darkest moment of the American Revolution, when the American army was starving and freezing at Valley Forge. His passionate words illustrate Washington's perseverance and *resolve* in the face of overwhelming odds against both the weather and the British army.

How bad were the conditions? New York's Gouverneur Morris of the Continental Congress wrote, "An army of skeletons appeared before our eyes naked, starved, sick and discouraged." The Marquis de Lafayette wrote: "The unfortunate soldiers were in want of everything; they had neither coats nor hats, nor shirts, nor shoes. Their feet and their legs froze until they were black, and it was often necessary to amputate them."

This "circular letter" was actually sent to all the states except Georgia and noted Washington's great urgency at a time when he was sorely discouraged. It reveals a shocking yet compassionate description of the plight of his troops. Washington also wrote stern but measured warnings of the consequences of failure if the troops did not receive adequate supplies soon.

While encamped at Valley Forge, Washington noted "how deficient—how exceedingly short they are of the complement of men which . . . they ought to have." Washington then proceeded to detail the urgent need for additional troops and supplies. He passionately pleaded with the New Hampshire legislature to take "early and vigorous measures" to raise more men. The outcome of the war, he stressed, depended on it. There is no doubt that Washington was deeply discouraged at this point of the war. Sadly, Congress and the States responded slowly to his requests, but the army remained committed to the cause. In spite of many challenges, Washington successfully rallied his troops and eventually won the war.

Clara Barton founded the American Red Cross in 1877, but she faced many trials and frustrations along the way. Early in life, she taught school in New Jersey, but she left the profession after a bitter personal disappointment. When a new school was built in Bordentown, New Jersey, Barton felt she had earned the right to become principal. The job went to a man instead.

Barton struggled with shyness most of her life. She was criticized for being an unmarried woman with a strong will and leadership qualities at a time when it was not culturally acceptable for a woman to behave in such a way. Even as a nurse, she had her critics. She faced many detractors for treating soldiers from *both* the North and South during the American Civil War. After founding the Red Cross, some board members publicly complained about her lack of record keeping skills. Barton too experienced episodes of discouragement and dissatisfaction. In spite of the *obstacles* she faced both personally and professionally, Clara Barton founded and nurtured an organization that has brought relief and encouragement to millions of people.

Disappointment is Natural

Personal struggle and feelings of disappointment are typical of what we all experience at certain difficult times in our lives. If you are suffering from deep depression or chronic discouragement however, I encourage you to seek professional medical advice.

So what can we do when everything *seems* to go wrong? What should we remember during these times? What can we do now to prepare for them?

First, understand that these chapters are part of the natural cycle of human life and can actually be beneficial if we keep these experiences in proper perspective. As people, we tend to exclusively focus on the short-term. We realize life is short and fragile, and there is a common tendency to view everything and every event in a short-term perspective. This is a mistake because short-term and long-term results are often very different. Worse yet, the outcome of short-term vs. long-term results are often the opposite of one another. This is true even though they were caused from the very same event.

The passing of time has a way of *changing* perspectives or reality. Not wearing that automotive seat belt may seem like a good idea when you are in a hurry or only traveling a short distance . . . until your car is involved in an accident. Telling a lie may seem like a good answer to avoid embarrassment until others later confront us with the facts. Exaggerating our tax deductions may seem wise until we receive notification of an audit. Many attractive physical pleasures seem enjoyable in the short-term, but the end results may be expensive, painful or addictive. The short-term can often *seem* right only because it is the easy or attractive route. But as the journey continues, it proves to be a dead-end road.

Analogy From a Gardener

As an amateur gardener and landscaper, I often see homeowners make expensive mistakes by focusing only on the short-term. A new homeowner usually wants to add color and plant life to their landscape as quickly as possible. So they go to the local nursery and purchase trees or shrubs to add natural color around the home. However, instead of planting and spacing this beautiful flora appropriately to accommodate their adult size, they will often plant them far too close together to fill up the existing space. Having only a short-term perspective results in these trees or bushes soon growing into each other and stunting their growth. This eventually forces the homeowner to remove some or all of them. The same is true of most decisions in life. The short-term perspective appears to be best and may actually work, at least for a while. But the effects of time change or *negate* the short-term results. Author Ernest Fitzgerald reminds us, "Triumphs are not always lasting and defeats are not always permanent." He continues by stating, "Everyone has been sometimes up and sometimes down, but few people have known which was which at the time . . . everyday may not be a good day but if you hang on, things have a way of changing. Somehow right things float to the surface. It helps to remember that when the news coming in is all bad."

During times of real discouragement, when everything seems to go wrong, we tend to have a special affinity for the short-term. Depressed emotions direct us to focus on the way we feel and hurt *right now*. While in these situations, we must become aware of this tendency. We must remind ourselves that these feelings are also only short-term. Tomorrow will be another day, and we must not overwhelm our emotional energy by the way we only feel at the moment. As we say in the gardening world, "Compost happens."

Recently, I purchased a *service* contract from a retail store. I noticed a comment near the end of the agreement. The remark stated that contrary to everything they just assured me in writing, their service is "subject to change without notice." If you are doing the right things with a sincere motive and positive attitude, you can be sure that just as suddenly as things may go wrong, they can also improve. So the next time something seriously goes wrong, tell yourself that this too "is subject to change without notice."

The right perspective to have is to accept the difficult situation at hand but look forward toward tomorrow, expecting the situation to change in the near future. In other words, look beyond the present situation and into the future. What should our approach be if it doesn't change tomorrow? Rest assured that you are now one day closer to a solution or change for the better.

This may also be a good time to candidly review your personal mission statement. Are we on the right mission, or did we deviate? Have we maintained our values and goals, or did we sacrifice them? If we discover we have deviated from our original mission or our values, it is time for some *serious* self-examination. Maybe this episode of despondency has been caused by an internal conflict over our mission, goals, or values. It is times like these when many great achievers have tapped into the religious, moral or ethical foundation of their souls to find comfort or seek direction. George Washington was humble enough to kneel in prayer and seek Divine intervention at Valley Forge.

If we have maintained our original values, we may simply be experiencing the short-term results of a temporary event that will improve with the passing of time. What else can we do when everything seems to go wrong?

What Can We Do When Discouraged

What should we remember during times of discouragement? Eventually, everyone has his or her dreams fractured. Very few people live without periods of self-doubt, severe problems or personal defeat. But personal leaders are those who *refuse* to stay down when they go down. Those who choose to lead are those who look back and remember their dreams and ideals. The core of personal leadership inspires one to maintain his or her deep inner vision of a better self, family, organization, business, or society. This is especially true in challenging times. We should always remember that every great achievement accomplished by the human race has been through hard struggle and great resistance. It is also during these times that we should draw strength from our families, friends, or mentors. I have personally found it encouraging to read the biographies of great leaders or achievers in history when I am discouraged. Their lives can remind us of the importance of personal endurance and determination against great odds. Legendary football coach Vince Lombardi summed it up when he said, "It doesn't matter how many times you get knocked down, but how many times you get up."

What can we do to prepare in advance for times of discouragement or despondency? Those who make it during the most difficult times are those who knowingly, or even unknowingly, prepared themselves in advance. During the stable and calm times, they established their convictions and fixed their values. It was during the peaceful moments that they decided that people are more important than possessions. They decided that a clear conscience is of greater value than increased profits, and integrity is worth more than dishonest glory. Those who desire to do great things have tested and *established* these values during the "good days." Then, when the valleys of life are later traveled, the momentum of those deep convictions pulls them through . . . upward toward the horizon. Those who stand in the "dark valleys" don't surrender because they decided—*long before*—what they believe and why. Propelled by the momentum of their values, they walk through the dark valleys until the landscape rises once again and dawn begins to break.

Lasting Success Comes From the Inside Out

The greatest possessions of our lives are not those things we discover or embrace on the outside, but what we discover within ourselves. It is during the times when "everything seems to go wrong" that we are jolted to reexamine who and what we are. It is also during these times that our beliefs and very purpose may be greatly challenged. As a personal leader, recognize that these times have the potential to make us more mature, stronger and wiser. Self-examination and a *reaffirmation* of our visions and values are powerful tools to combat discouragement. I encourage you to view the difficult times in your life from a long-term perspective. Don't allow your feelings of disappointment today to *cloud* your trust in a better tomorrow.

But what if you are going through a disappointment so severe you feel like a "failure"? What if others even refer to you as a failure? What if you feel that things couldn't possibly get any worse? Failure is a *strong* word. It even sounds harsh and judgmental. In the Western world, it is often applied to people in a condescending way. It is also typically used in a way that emphasizes permanence. When someone is *labeled* a failure, it is often implied that he or she has little value and that there is no opportunity to change his or her situation. When an event is called a failure, it is often implied that the results were miserable and unchangeable. But is this really the correct definition of this impolite word? Is this the proper perspective for a leader to have?

Time Can Turn Failure into Success

First of all, a failure is relative to time. How do we know we have had a *good* or *bad* day? The answer is often relative to the passing of time. Sometimes we may believe we have had an excellent day only to find out later that something else was going on we didn't know was occurring. When we analyze the day in its entirety from hindsight, it turns out to be different than we first thought. On the other hand, we have all had days that seemed to be very bad. Maybe everything appeared to go very wrong, or the day had a single large event that turned it into a negative image. Yet, when we were given some *exciting news* later that evening, it may have turned out to be the best thing that ever happened to us.

Time turns a lot of failures into successes. The first great American general was George Washington. But early in the American Revolutionary War, few would have called him even adequate, let alone great. He lost virtually every battle and skirmish against the British troops, and *retreat* was common. He and his men were demoralized, and at times it appeared the war was lost. Yet time proved these battles had just the right effect. The British resolve to keep the American colonies was being diminished with each battle and with the loss of every British soldier. It turned out that winning battles was not as important as the resolve to continue . . . no matter what *appeared* to be happening. Time transformed George Washington from a failure to a hero. The same is true in our lives.

We must often be prepared to patiently wait for our efforts to produce results we *can* see. It is easy to do something and expect immediate results. We may even suspect failure has occurred if we don't quickly see something tangible happen. But remember that seeds sprout underground *before* you can see them. Sometimes they grow slowly and first establish *roots* before we see any tangible evidence of life. Those of us who garden regularly learn to wait patiently for the flowers to bloom. In the same way, we must be careful not to casually judge an action or event as a failure. It is very possible that not enough time has elapsed to correctly judge the results. This same principle that holds true in nature is also true in life.

Don't Judge by Short-term Events

The second thing about failure is that it is relative to your limited perspective. Something terrible may happen in your life, but with patience and a closer examination, you may clearly see a "silver lining."

The perception of life at any given moment may not reveal its *true* meaning. Most of us make the mistake of judging events too quickly or with too little evidence. If we judge ourselves (or others) by too few circumstances, we will incorrectly label an entire life by only a few isolated events. Perhaps just another day away, or over the next obstacle, we will be able to view what appeared to be a failure as a true success. The people who win are those who hold on to their hopes and dreams. They patiently wait for the proper perspective to become clear.

Many folks feel like failures because they don't have the right standards to measure success or failure. They have allowed the media to define what success is and is not. However, success is not the achievement of power, prestige or great influence. Some individuals achieve these goals but are not happy or even content with what they have. Numerous athletes and entertainers achieve these things only to lose it all in a lifestyle of self-destruction. Success is doing what you can, wherever you are, with whatever you have. Achieving our best is always limited by our existing circumstances. It is easy to say, "If only I had known, or if only I could turn back the hands of time." But we simply can't do that because no one can know everything. Hindsight is 20/20, but the future is always hazy. We all have to make decisions and plot our direction with only the information and resources we presently have at hand.

Many years ago, a young, struggling cartoonist lost his job when he was told by his boss "he couldn't draw and had no talent." He decided to work for himself and find his own clients. After a long period of struggle and apparent failure, he found only one customer! A minister paid him a very small amount of money to draw advertising for his church. The cartoonist was so downtrodden and pathetic the church allowed him to stay in their mouse-infested garage. While he lived there, he drew cartoons that no one seemed to want, and nicknamed his favorite little mouse who scurried about the garage floor—Mickey Mouse.

From apparent failure, Walt Disney transcended disappointment and misfortune to become a success. He achieved this by believing in his vision, overcoming disappointment and living his mission with a right perspective. Remember to maintain the *long*-term perspective the next time you get discouraged and everything seems to be going wrong. Leaders aren't born, but they often rise out of adversity.

Recap of Principle #6

It is natural to go through times when everything seems to go wrong. When this occurs, realize that this too may have an important purpose in your life. Focus on your long-term goals, and don't sacrifice your core values or abandon your mission when you are discouraged. If you have prepared in advance, the momentum of those deep convictions will pull you through toward a new and brighter day. Be careful how you define a "failure" and how quickly you make this judgment about yourself or others. Yes, when we feel we have "missed the mark" or *failed*, we should seriously examine what we did wrong to learn from the experience. But remember that failure is relative to time. What may appear to be a failure today may plant the seeds for success tomorrow. Secondly, failure is often success when we see it from a *different* point of view. With a proper perspective, what actually happens in the "end" may be far different than what we immediately see.

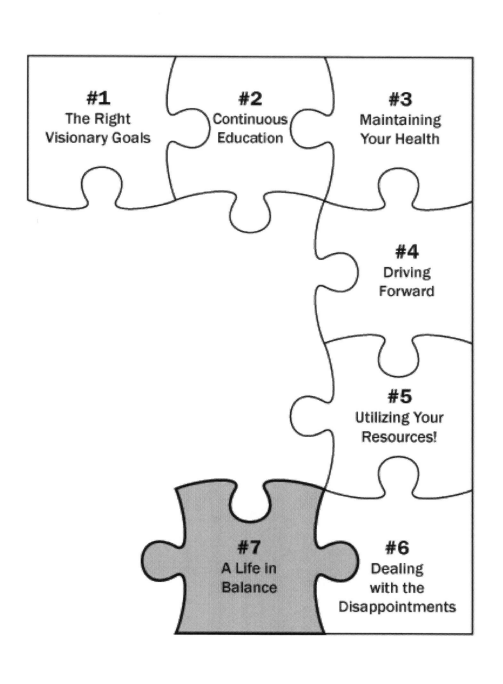

PRINCIPLE #7

<u>A LIFE IN BALANCE</u>

Recently, I was reading about a woman who won the New Jersey state lottery twice. She won once in 1985 and again in 1986 for a total of 5.4 million U.S. dollars. Do you think she is living on easy street? Perhaps she spends her days in grand comfort using her money to make the world a better place for the *less* fortunate? No, the money is gone, and she lives in a trailer home. Another man won 16.2 million U.S. dollars in the 1988 Pennsylvania lottery. After a series of bad investments and bad personal relationships, his wealth quickly ended. Within a year, he was one million dollars in debt, and he lives today on a monthly $450 Social Security check and food stamps provided by the government. Recently, in my home state of Ohio, the widow of a former lottery winner was interviewed by a local newspaper. She told the sad story of her former husband turning into an alcoholic and destroying his life and health after winning the lottery. She stated that if you already have serious problems, money only makes those problems bigger.

Perhaps you have read or heard similar scenarios hundreds of times. I am sure you could name an actor, athlete, politician or religious figure who appeared to have it all. They struggled for many years to develop the skills needed to get to the top. They had a burning desire to be the best. They appeared to "pay their dues" and seemed to make a total commitment to reach the pinnacle of their craft. Then, when it seemed they had climbed to the top of the mountain and finally achieved their lifetime goal of celebrity, wealth, power, or prestige . . . it happened. A fatal personal flaw suddenly exploded to bring them down like a house of cards! For some, it may be a life-altering addiction or a blatant lack of integrity. For others, it may be outright hypocrisy or a self-absorbed ego that has led them to believe they are now *above* the law and justice that everyone else is expected to live by. Whatever the reasons or excuses given, they all have one important thing in common.

In spite of their talents and abilities, they lacked an essential principle needed to preserve success. That principle is establishing and maintaining a life in proper balance. *Encarta Dictionary* offers a definition of balance as "a state in which various elements form a satisfying and harmonious whole and nothing is out of proportion or unduly emphasized at the expense of the rest."

Even though I travel a lot, often overnight, I have learned the importance of balance. When away from home, I will usually take a walk in the evening to get some exercise or clear my mind. I also like to visit old historical cemeteries. I remind myself that compared to the underground tenants, things might not be so bad after all. In over thirty years of travel, I have called home virtually every night to connect with my wife and family. I take varied reading material with me so I don't waste an entire evening watching television in a hotel room. I have learned to enjoy a variety of these little pleasures while I am at home or on the road. The spice of life is learning to balance many small, positive activities rather than being addicted or obsessed about one or two things.

Personal Leadership Can Make a Difference

Remember, personal leadership is the desire of individuals to take charge of their own lives. They realize that leadership is not a position or title but an outlook on life and *their* role in the world. Like most things, "balance" does not come easily to most people. If it did, the individuals discussed in the opening paragraphs would have had it, and their stories would be different. Living a philosophy of personal leadership does not require a magical formula. Nor is it available to only a few. It is actually available to most folks, but what it requires is a deep commitment to balance, a sense of purpose and values. The plain truth is that most people are unwilling to make this kind of commitment because it requires self-discipline and personal sacrifice. If personal leadership had a motto, it would be this: "Before I seek to change or motivate others, I must first learn to change and motivate myself." Mahatma Gandhi said, "We must become the *change* we want to see." In this way, personal leadership is also about becoming a good follower. We subject ourselves to the morals and ethics we claim to believe. We learn to follow our own consciences as we seek continuous improvement. We then correct our courses when convicted of a need for change.

Personal leaders have a *game plan* for their lives. Call it what you will, a personal mission statement, life strategic plan, setting of goals or a personal punch list. It is a road map designed to give your life direction or to establish a clear path for your life. Unfortunately, most people live their lives like a raft floating in the ocean. They bob up and down, left and right, over and under, depending on the tempest of the sea and their environment. They become victims of circumstance and allow time to make decisions they are unwilling to make for themselves. In contrast, personal leaders are absolutely convinced they have a great degree of control over their own circumstances and outcomes. They are not about to leave their futures in the hands of *time and chance*. The sea change they experience is the one that leads them to learn something new because they have decided to make it a part of their lives. Just like athletes (or their teams) need a game plan to excel, so do we. A mental leap *forward* comes when we take the vague ideas and goals rolling around in our head and put them on paper as a personal mission statement. When done correctly and reviewed often, it has the potential to intensify our focus and increase our desire for achievement at a higher level.

The 7ᵗʰ Principle Defined

Now we come to the next vital principle that holds our lives together like natural glue. Without a life in balance, all the previous principles will only get us so far, and we may achieve a high level of success or fulfillment, for a while. But, if we allow our lives to become *imbalanced* by nurturing or tolerating addictions, obsessions, or neglect, we will eventually flush it all down the drain. Why do we need balance? Life is a complex mixture of personal needs and responsibilities. When disharmony occurs in life it will eventually cause serious problems. An automobile tire provides an example of the need for balance. It is designed to function effectively when it is balanced properly. It is often under great stress in its environment. If it becomes imbalanced, the result is excessive wear and a shortened lifespan. In the worst case, an imbalanced tire can cause a blowout and literally fail while the car is on the road. The same can hold true for us. We too, are designed to function effectively when in balance. Like a tire, we also experience great stress, and living an uneven existence will shorten our life. Eventually, given enough stress and emotional wear, a person will also breakdown.

Many of the folks who win the lottery, as well as many celebrities, were already living imbalanced lives when "success" suddenly appeared. Some were already addicted to drugs, alcohol, spending or sex before the money and glamour arrived. Others were incapable of handling their meager finances before the riches materialized. All that the notoriety and cash did was aggravate a dysfunction and accelerate it. A lack of balance was the Achilles heel in their lives. To those who lack balance, another *negative* consequence of wealth is the ability to "try" new things now that they have enough money to afford it.

An *addiction* to any kind of substance or activity makes us a slave to the craving. We are not happy unless we feed it again and again. After a period of time, it consumes our thoughts and energies. It becomes the primary thing we need and think about. We are unhappy and unsettled if we don't have it. An addiction takes over your life, and you begin to neglect other areas that need and deserve attention. For example, something as seemingly innocuous as cigarette smoking can have very negative consequences. It makes the individual who smokes smell foul. It is unhealthy to the smoker and those who are around the toxic air produced. It is controlling and addictive in two different ways. The *psychological* addiction causes you to feel content only if you have something in your mouth. The *physical* addiction is the craving for more nicotine. In business, I have often been amazed to see people flee out of a meeting in a panic because they "need a cigarette" to feed their craving for nicotine.

Addictions and Obsessions Are Destructive

An obsession is when we spend too much thought and time on any one thing. It may not be as destructive as a physical addiction, but it can have the same effect. For example, being a *workaholic* is an obsession. Many who become workaholics do so because they falsely believe they can find meaning or achievement in their work. Others are trying to avoid doing something else they should be doing. Of itself, work is a good thing and can be fulfilling. However, when we become consumed with "work" or becoming "successful," we neglect our family and friends. We then sow the seeds of destroying our personal relationships and neglect our responsibilities. These include family, work, recreation, spirituality, community and self-fulfillment. They all require a certain degree of attention and nurturing. If this doesn't happen, an imbalance occurs in life.

An imbalanced life results from not providing the right mixture of resources to every personal need just mentioned. We are finite beings, and our personal resources are limited. When one area of life consumes most of our energies, thoughts, time and attention—instability occurs and eventually it becomes the norm. Allow me to use an analogy to make my point.

Modern Analogy From Microsoft Windows®

If you have ever worked on a computer that has a Microsoft Windows® operating system, you know exactly what I mean about limited resources. This popular software program interacts with the computer hardware and allows it to become a working PC or personal computer. Combined together, this interaction between software and hardware is designed to be compatible, and one result is referred to as *system* resources. Depending on the motherboard design, CPU, random access memory (RAM), and other design qualities, system resources are limited. Even with a large hard drive and abundant RAM, resources can still be limited because of the way the operating system is designed. For example, sometimes I have a word processor, spreadsheet, web browser, e-mail program, FTP program and file manager all open at the same time on my PC. While I am working on one, the others are still *minimized* in the background and taking up system resources. Another example includes all the other software programs that automatically load themselves in Windows when it is booted. These individual programs may take up little memory, but together they can consume a lot of resources. When this happens, the PC slows down. If it doesn't have enough RAM, it may even swap some of the memory onto the hard drive. Because so many resources are utilized, switching from one program to another may cause the system to become unstable, resulting in the infamous "blue screen of death."

It is not my intent to criticize the most popular operating system on earth or point out its flaws. So what does all of this information about the Windows operating system have to do with *balance*? It can give us a lot to think about as we apply this information and draw an analogy to ourselves. Just like PC's, we also have very precious and limited resources. To maintain a balance in life, we need to allocate those finite resources effectively. At times, this means knowing what to maximize and what should receive full attention. This also means we know what other areas to minimize while being able to shift and balance sudden needs and responsibilities. Anything in life that becomes an addiction or obsession depletes our ability to do this. Serious dysfunctional behavior robs precious resources needed to balance other areas in life.

Maintain a Needed Balance in Life

Here are a few things to consider to help you maintain a needed balance in your life.

Do you have an addiction or obsession? If so, please stop living in denial and get some help. Don't be too proud or stubborn to get the professional help you need right away. Please don't jeopardize all you have achieved or could achieve by continuing to live like a slave to something that has gotten out of control. Also, confide in a friend or loved one, and ask them to help you through the process of breaking this destructive habit or lifestyle.

Another area that needs genuine balance is our communication skills. Human beings were created to be sociable and interactive. I believe that the ability to communicate well is a developed trait which requires much effort and practice from most of us. Allow me to provide you with a few "tips" on how to increase effective communication. Remember, your positive relationships with your spouse, children, relatives, friends, employer and co-workers rest on your ability to verbalize and *listen* well.

Five Communication Tips

1) **Be approachable and friendly.** Show others that you are really interested in what they have to say. Stop what you are doing to focus on what they are saying. Look into their eyes to reveal that you are concentrating on what is being said. Smile and give a positive feeling of acknowledgement in the way you respond. Be an active listener, and ask some questions if you don't *understand* what is being stated. Don't just assume you understand a remark which is unclear. Occasionally repeat back to others what you heard them say to show you are listening. Asking questions also shows others you are listening and trying to understand.

2) **Be personable and animated in your response.** Allow others to finish their remarks before you speak. Don't cut them off in mid-sentence. Don't think about what you are *going to say* while they are still speaking to you. When you respond, show life and animation in your comments. Use humor when appropriate—especially if there is a need to reduce tension.

3) **Show *positive* body language.** Express relaxed gestures that show your interest in the conversation. Kinesics is the study of communication through body movement. We may be able to hide our feelings through what we say, but they are usually *revealed* through our body language. Actions such as lowering your head in your hand, rolling your eyes, folding your arms or looking aimlessly into space may contradict the words you are saying. Analyze the gestures you make during conversation. Train yourself to eliminate the "I don't really care or agree" gestures and replace them with "I'm really interested" body language.

4) **Practice flexibility and *tact*.** No one likes to talk to someone who is dogmatic about *everything* and insensitive to other people's feelings. Be open-minded to other ideas and thoughts. Avoid the use of "gunpowder words" like (you) *always, never, all*, and *everytime*. Replace

these exaggerated words with softer expressions like *many, often, seldom* or *usually*. Don't come across as arrogant or as a know-it-all because you will lose respect and credibility.

If you disagree with a statement, demonstrate your disapproval with grace and respect for the person. It is possible to disagree without being harsh or disagreeable. Politeness and respect toward others is essential to effective two-way conversation. The key is to be open and honest, and be sure you don't make your disagreement a personal attack.

5) **Express genuine empathy and concern for others.** Don't be condescending or act superior to other people. When someone approaches you with a problem, show a genuine *attitude* of concern. Listen to them, patiently hear them out, and offer support. If appropriate, also offer your insight and advice. Let them know their problems are of concern to you. Don't hesitate to use sincere phrases like: "I'm sorry to hear that. Is there anything I can do to help?" Thinking sympathetically is not the same as *acting* and speaking with empathy. The purpose of effective communication is to "build bridges" of understanding to one another, not to build walls of isolation.

Here are a couple of humorous examples that I suggest you avoid saying.

American sardonic writer Dorothy Parker was once asked by an annoying guest at a party if she had ever had her ears pierced. Parker replied, "No, but I have often had them bored."

I believe it was Groucho Marx (in one of his comedy skits) who once told a dinner host upon leaving their home, "I have truly had a wonderful evening—but this wasn't it."

Develop Your Communication Skills

Unfortunately, we were not naturally born with the ability to communicate well, especially in sensing the needs of others. It doesn't come by human instinct or with a formal education. Animals have little need for this type of interpersonal communication. Most of what they know is acquired from instinct or in the earliest stages of animal life. Animals have brains to assist them in their survival. However, we humans have the need to grow far beyond our own instinct, which can be extremely selfish. We have minds which were designed to *transcend* the limited ability of a mere physical brain.

In comparison to animals, we humans are born with limited instincts, such as nursing and reflex reactions. We also were not born with an "owner's manual" to program us to be immediately useful and effective. Many of the great religions were created to provide a manual for productive living because we simply lack any other purpose upon birth except for basic survival. As far as we know, the mental ability to robustly communicate, reason, design, and *aspire* to greatness is limited to human beings on this planet. For decades, scientists have been sending communication signals into space hoping for an audible reply from another world. To date—there is no response from anywhere in the universe.

Here is an activity I strongly encourage you to consider. Why not join or start a local *speech* club in your community? This is a great way to sharpen your talents, meet new people, and enrich your life. There is a major reason I encourage you to do this. A speech club will help you to master one of the most valuable traits any person can acquire and one that leaders absolutely need. This is the ability to effectively communicate with others individually and in groups. Communication is a two-way process in which people seek to gain a greater understanding of the ideas of others. This is done by listening to and sharing thoughts, feelings, and needs.

Think for a moment how important this trait really is. How many jobs are lost, conflicts created and opportunities denied because of the inability to communicate well? How much creative talent in others goes untapped because a leader won't listen to followers? How many marriages have been eroded because someone was not able to really communicate their feelings and ideas? How many people have misunderstood another's real needs because of a lack of communication? How many child-rearing problems exist because of a lack of listening? I think you get the point. Most of humankind's problems exist because we really don't make a *serious* effort or take the time to communicate with each other. When folks go to professional counselors for help to solve relationship problems, the professionals spend much of their time teaching people *how* to communicate in order to resolve personal conflicts.

How to Correct Others Effectively

But what if the situation calls upon you to correct or reprimand another person? How can we do this in a balanced way that is effective? This is an unpleasant task which all leaders must do occasionally. Obviously, if the only time you spend talking with people is to *correct* them, you will get severe resistance from them leading to bitterness. Why? Because you have lost trust and credibility with them. When others see you daily providing encouragement and praise toward them, it is easier and more effective when you do need to correct them.

Here's how to do it properly and get positive results. Begin by *complimenting* the individual, telling the person about the things they are doing right. Openly acknowledge and express how pleased you are about the good things they do. Show appreciation for the ways they contribute to others. Give them specific examples of some things they do well, not vague generalities.

Next, follow this praise with a few sentences of brief correction. Be calm and reasoned. Express that you are disappointed in their *actions* and not in them. Explain exactly what you desire to see in the future and why it is important. Lastly, end your conversation by showing more appreciation and encouragement for the fine things they do. Explain that you have confidence in them to accomplish and grow even more. Make sure you end the discussion on a *positive* note, not a confrontational one.

If you don't do this perfectly, or if you struggle with this task, welcome to the club. As I mentioned earlier, we not only need formal book knowledge, we all need to develop enhanced leadership, character and personality skills. These traits cannot be taught through a formal education or by reading a book. They must be acquired by *life* experience and reinforced by a desire for personal excellence!

Get Away From It All

Are you on the verge of *becoming* a workaholic? Take a number of scheduled breaks during the day and clear your mind. During these breaks, spend a few minutes to think about enjoyable activities away from the work environment. The mind is like a battery that needs to be reenergized regularly to remain highly charged and able to focus effectively. Take your scheduled lunch break to recharge your mind. Take a walk or short drive to change environments for a while. Don't eat at your desk when you are supposed to be on a lunch break. It is counterproductive and is a warning sign of possible meltdown if changes are not made. You will be much more productive if you refresh your mind and take scheduled breaks during the day.

Another important way to nurture your personal resources is to take a vacation regularly. I believe this is not only important annually but also on a weekly basis. More and more physicians and mental health professionals are emphasizing the tremendous importance of taking at least one day off every week. Again, the human mind and body needs a period of rest and relaxation. A few years ago, a friend of mine told me he hadn't taken a vacation in three years. I thought, "Who are you trying to impress?"

Learn to become aware of your body's *warning* signs of stress. These may include a tense jaw, stiff neck, headache, or the feeling of being overwhelmed. When any of these signs begin to occur, its time for an immediate break. Then ask yourself some heartfelt questions. Think about the possible root cause of the stress. Are there any small tasks you are holding on to that you can delegate? Are you making *more* out of an obstacle or problem than is really there? Is there another co-worker with expertise available to help? Are you feeling stressed out because of time restraints or the responsibility of too many tasks? Think the situation through, and you will see there are always some good options. The worst thing you can do is panic or overreact.

Get into a weekly habit of communing with mother earth. This beautiful creation exists for a reason, and spending time outdoors is therapeutic. Dr. Andrew Weil promotes and suggests forty-five minutes of walking or jogging at least five days a week. So take a long walk regularly, work in the yard, or play some sports with the family. In other words, get more active and step away from the sedentary lifestyle too many of us are now in due to work environments, television and the Internet. This has mental as well as physical benefits. As Stephen Covey reminds us, it is important to take the time to "sharpen the saw." I will discuss this in more detail in the next chapter.

Recap of Principle #7

Remember, your personal resources are limited and precious. To achieve the things you desire and to *maintain* them, you must live a life in balance with your needs and responsibilities. This means taking efforts to minimize stress and experiencing refreshing diversions daily, weekly and annually. The way you express yourself and communicate to others also needs to be pleasant and balanced.

Personal leaders know they must get professional help when they become aware of an addiction or controlling obsession. Just as an imbalanced automobile tire can cause uneven wear and a blowout, a neglected or overlooked personal dysfunction can cause a blowout in your life. Take time throughout the day and week to allow your mind to be refreshed. As leadership author and consultant Paul Thornton states it, "Be the leader, make the difference."

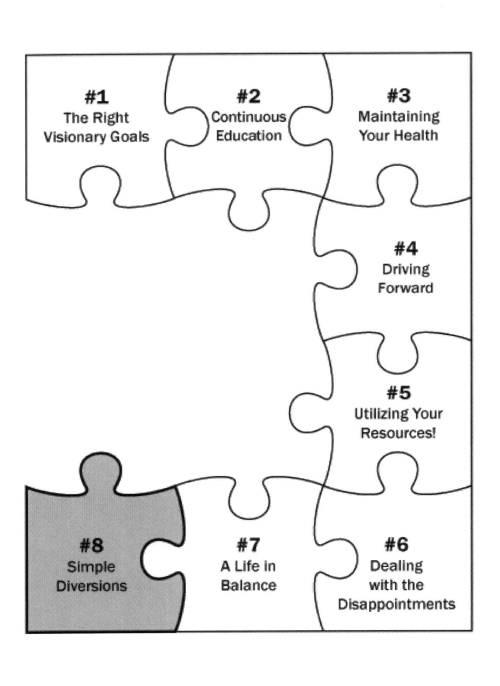

PRINCIPLE #8

SIMPLE DIVERSIONS

As I mentioned earlier, by the time I graduated from high school in the early 1970s, I had been prepared to enter the construction industry as an electrician. It had been determined by school authorities that I did not have college potential. In those days, students were both labeled and categorized where the school officials determined they should be. Males who were not designated as "college material" had limited options. A student's career was then directed toward auto repair shop, art classes or one of the construction trades. I did not disappoint the school administrators or the low expectations that they had about me. I was unmotivated and uninspired to achieve in a high school environment.

After working for an uncle for a number of months in the auto reconditioning business, my first real job was as an apprentice electrician at age eighteen. In one of my early experiences, I was sent to do electrical work at the private home of a noted business executive. "Mr. Fischer" was the president and driving innovator of a major international corporation that manufactured conveyor systems and monorails. He lived in an exclusive area of Northern Ohio known as Waite Hill. This was a small, wealthy and exclusive community in Lake County, Ohio, that had a population of fewer than 500 people. Within this small town were a number of mansions and incredible properties located in a genteel and quiet environment. As a young man who grew up in the modest middle-class streets of Cleveland, I was stunned by the magnificence of his home and property.

Aside from his actual residence, what I remember most about his homestead was the impressive *recreational* building located on the large property. It included a central clubhouse with full kitchen facilities and bath house. Walking out of one side of this building, you were led to a full-size tennis court that was surfaced immaculately and with the exact proportions of a professional court. If you walked out of the other side of this opulent clubhouse, you would enter into a pristine swimming pool area. The pool was surrounded with beautiful cabana furniture and lounge chairs. Of course, the entire clubhouse area was impeccably landscaped, just like the rest of the property.

Sad Story of Mr. Fischer

Due to my electrical work on the property, I struck up a few conversations with the maintenance man of the property. He was employed by Mr. Fischer to oversee the entire complex and make sure the buildings and grounds were maintained well and according to his instructions. "Scotty" was a portly man who usually wore a dirty and drab olive green maintenance uniform. He was a jovial and friendly man who worked on the property about twelve hours a day and virtually seven days a week. He was always "on-call" in case something went wrong on the property. He had faithfully worked for Mr. Fischer for many years and was well liked by everyone who knew him. One day in a conversation with Scotty, I asked him how often Mr. Fischer used his clubhouse and tennis court or pool. His answer shocked me, and I will never forget his reply. He said, "I have worked for Mr. Fischer for many years. Most mornings I am here at 6:00 AM to start my day, and by the time I get here, he has *already* left for the office. Usually, I leave at sunset and he has not returned from the office. I also work here on most weekends, and I can tell you that I have *never* seen Mr. Fischer use the tennis court or swimming pool!"

That was my first experience with someone who was addicted to work and a proverbial workaholic. Here was a wealthy industrialist who on the outside appeared to have it all. He had a company of his own, majestic property, beautiful wife, European sports car, money, prestige and power. What he didn't have was a meaningful life. I wondered to myself what the purpose of this magnificent home and property was if he never enjoyed it. Then it dawned on me that this home and other possessions were only a *trophy* for him. It was an image to others that he had made it to the top of the business world. He didn't even take the time to enjoy it because he was addicted to work. Sadly, a few years later Mr. Fischer was indicted for a serious felony regarding fraud and tax evasion. He took his own life rather than face the consequences of his actions and crime. Thus ended the cheerless story of Mr. Fischer. I had not thought of him for many years until a commercial was run on television a few years ago. As I remember, it was sponsored by a financial company encouraging the viewers to prepare for their retirement.

The commercial emphasized how we all get so wrapped up in work and our problems that we forget to *live*. It boldly proclaimed, "While you were out, life called, and you're late."

The human mind is a remarkable organ, and it was designed to accomplish multiple and challenging tasks. What we often fail to realize is that it was also designed to be *refreshed* by enjoying recreation on a regular basis. You may have heard the old saying that, "All work and no play makes for a dull boy." In truth, it makes one worse than a dull boy. In time it will make one a self-absorbed, miserable person with few real friends and a lack of real fulfillment. The problem with being obsessed with work or accomplishments is that whatever you do finish, or accomplish never seems to be enough. This psychological disease is very deceptive because the amount of productivity or success you achieve is always outstripped by what *still* lies ahead and is yet waiting to be done. One becomes so busy achieving, there is no room left for enjoying and savoring the life we have been given.

New Research on Stress

Recent cutting-edge research on stress and worry is very revealing. Stress causes heart rates and blood pressure to rise. It contributes to a weakened immune system, surges of stress hormones that strain heart tissue, and eventually causes depression. Worrying or continually mulling over our problems produces the same results. Many health care providers refer to this as "overthinking," and it appears that humans are the only species prone to this problem. But the research also found that people who force themselves to *step away* from a stressful environment and perform diversionary tasks return to their original healthy levels more quickly than those who continue to be stressed or over-think things. Dr. Nicholas Christenfeld of the University of California-San Diego has been involved in recent studies on worry and stress. As a psychologist, he has observed in his studies that people who are stressed out, and perform either vigorous exercise or listen to music speed up the physical recovery needed after experiencing stress. He believes that *distraction* may prevent the harmful effects of mental stress or worry in the short term.

However, in our modern world it seems that diverting ourselves from the daily pressures of living is more difficult than ever. We have telephones, cell phones, e-mail, voicemail, the Internet and dozens of new technologies to absorb our time. The traditional forty-hour work week has greatly expanded for many workers. Even when they are at home for the evening, there is e-mail to be checked and answered, memos or reports to review, more work than ever to be done. Combined with this is a myriad of other personal tasks that demand our time. There are financial responsibilities, health needs, family demands, and community obligations. It seems like the pressures grow day-by-day.

When we become so wrapped up in work or what we feel are our duties, we begin to miss out on the purpose of life. Your life is much more than work. We can build software and machines to do work. But we can't build software or machines that have a heart to enjoy family and friends. The most advanced software available can't lead us to find meaning in the world around us. No matter how important we may think we are, when we are gone, someone else will do our work. Many people are not *truly* living; they are "being lived" by society or a personal addiction. Within a generation or two, very few will remember or care about the work we allowed to consume our lives. Except for a few extraordinarily great leaders, 99.9 percent of everyone who has ever lived and their work has been unrecorded, underappreciated and forgotten. Does this mean we live our lives in vain? No, it doesn't, and we will discuss why in a later principle.

Why Diversions Are Important

Sadly, many people from all levels of our society have become comfortable with one-dimensional lives. They have become emotionally imbalanced because they are obsessed with work or music or sports or even religion. Of themselves, each of these activities are wonderful and can add a special dimension to life and make it more meaningful. However, when we become so deeply entrenched in *any* activity that we shut out joy, people, family, or other activities, we become warped in our perspective of what life is all about. This makes us self-centered, and it steals happiness and contentment from our souls. Lasting gratification is achieved when we share our lives with others. Only when we are interdependent with others can we tap deeply into the meaning of life. This is not possible when we isolate ourselves and live in our own little secluded worlds.

We all have a deep *need* to experience simple and refreshing diversions in our stress-filled lives to keep a proper perspective and maximize each day. Examples of this might include taking time to enjoy your family, playing some sports, walking to take pleasure in the local scenery, meditating, savoring your favorite hobbies, reading a good book, calling a friend to chat, or volunteering to serve others. There are many other ways you can deliberately set aside time to invigorate your thoughts, depending on your lifestyle and environment. The wonderful thing about these simple yet powerful distractions is that most are free. They don't cost anything except a dedicated commitment of *your time* to relish them.

So what is the solution to this dilemma? The answer is you must purposely *schedule* a number of meaningful distractions into your life, and these simple diversions must be considered as important as any other thing you do. These diversions should be enthusiastically utilized daily, weekly and seasonally.

The Incredible Potential of the Mind

Some scientists believe that the memory storage capacity of the human brain may be up to 1000 terabytes. I would like to give you an idea of how enormous this is. As an example, in May 2007, The U.S. Library of Congress Web Capture team claimed that "the entire Library has collected more than 70 terabytes of data." This equals only about 7 percent of what the human mind may be able to store.

It has been estimated that the average person only uses 10 percent of the capacity of their physical brain. What is the other 90 percent for? I believe it was provided for us to develop and grow through a wide variety of lifetime experiences and challenges. Years ago, I complimented a friend of mine on something new he had done; actually, he had performed it very well. His humorous reply to me was, "Are you kidding? I've got talents I haven't even discovered yet." This is true for all of us, but unfortunately most of us only learn enough to survive or to get slightly ahead of others. Earlier, I mentioned how my high school in the early 1970s categorized students into groups based on where the school officials thought we should fit in society. The truth is that every culture or society on earth attempts to do the same thing to you. There is a *default* position for you in society, depending on your family's social status, ethnicity, skin color, neighborhood, educational level, income level or influential connections. If you just go with the flow, you will end up there because it is where you are expected to fit by others.

Yet, once you determine to break through that limitation, you will immediately discover strong *resistance* because you are no longer playing by the unspoken rules. Unbelievably, this resistance often comes from those we love and trust the most. Because of defeatism or plain jealousy, some will resent our efforts to improve our lives. The blessing that the United States has been to the world is that it has offered the greatest opportunity for any individual to reach his or her highest potential regardless of birth status. The

American republic was founded on the concept of encouraging the "pursuit of happiness." However, it is our responsibility to *pursue* it.

Yet, why don't more people make an effort to change their lives and reach their greatest potential? For many people, the default position that society has established for them is comfortable and seems natural. If you are deeply content right where you are, there is little possibility of change or growth. What does all this have to do with simple diversions? More than you may think.

Again, if we *believe* we are where we are supposed to fit in, and are content with that role, we will usually stop learning and growing. Thus the human mind, with all of its extra capacity, will go undeveloped and remain void of new experiences or opportunities. By bringing into our lives a few simple diversions, we expand our knowledge and expertise about hobbies or studies that interest us. Obviously, these simple diversions should be positive and in concert with our values and morals.

My Personal Diversion

A number of years ago, I joined the American Rose Society (ARS). Because of my late mother's example, I have a deep love and interest in growing roses. I am not interested in exhibiting roses in shows or at local conventions, but I am interested in the cultivation and propagation of roses. This is one of *my* simple diversions, and I enjoy it immensely. After I joined the ARS and began to read its publications, I attended their annual Rose Show in Cleveland in 2001. The exhibition was beautiful, but I personally found the various seminars to be of the most interest to me. I also learned something that caught my attention. Many physicians and other professionals were avid members of the ARS. Why? Growing roses offered them a challenging and fulfilling way to release the stress of their careers when they went home. After a long, nerve-racking day of practicing medicine or law, they enjoyed coming out to the yard and cultivating their roses by spraying, fertilizing, trimming, or hybridizing these beautiful plants. Their reward is observing the slight changes that occur every day and having an assortment of beautiful roses in their yard, in their homes or at the exhibition hall. Since the great majority of ARS members are not doctors or lawyers, it is obvious that people from virtually every walk of life enjoy this simple diversion.

So what is *your* simple diversion? Perhaps it is fishing, scrapbooking, hiking, rubberstamping, stamp-collecting, woodworking, or one of hundreds of positive activities. When we participate in these diversions, they refresh our minds and bring pleasure because we enjoy spending time with them. But there is another benefit. Oftentimes, these so-called simple diversions can grow into passions that lead us to becoming experts in unique fields. They may even lead us to our true callings in other careers where we should have been all along.

You never know what your hobby or interest may lead to. Every year the *All-America Rose Selections* (AARS) are announced to the public. The AARS is an association of leading American wholesale growers and rose breeders. It supports a two-year rose trial in twenty gardens located in about every climate condition in the United States. Its goal is to draw attention to exceptional new roses that perform well. One of the 2008 award winners was named *Dream Come True*. This excellent rose was bred by an amateur rose breeder, a retired doctor who lives in Ohio. Remember an amateur is defined as someone who does something for pleasure rather than for pay. However, once we discover our passions, and do what we really love, it often leads to monetary rewards.

How Often Should We Take a Break?

How often are simple diversions necessary? First of all, we should take a number of them during the work day. We call them "breaks," and many people skip them because they want to be more productive. Actually, the opposite is true. Being focused on one single activity for too long can become monotonous and stifle creativity. In some careers, it can even become a safety hazard. In contrast, short breaks refresh our minds by changing our scenery and providing new smells or sounds or tastes to stimulate the brain. This gives our minds an opportunity to "reboot" so when we return to work we can have a fresh perspective.

We also need to have a weekly break. History shows that many advanced and productive cultures rested at least one day in a seven day week. The reason for this is simple. Humankind tends to have workaholic tendencies and will often overwork unless it stops to observe a day of rest from physical labors. Life is much more than work, and if we don't take time out to ponder the purpose of life and our role in it, we become *voluntary* slaves to a workaholic culture. As a child it was easier to take time to rest than it is today. In the 1960s, many areas of the United States had laws that virtually forced people to rest on Sunday. It was a *family day* for a large number of Americans as they gathered to attend religious observances, watch sporting events, play in the yard, and enjoy a large meal. Though I don't think anyone should be forced to cease working on a certain day in a democratic society, we have lost some important benefits in the decline of this practice. In the twenty-first century, it's all about making money and materialism. People work seven days a week because they can. They make the mistake of thinking that more money will provide them happiness or fulfillment. Many parents falsely believe that working obsessively to buy more material things will show their children that they love them. Actually, spending time with them in family play, conversation, dining or worship will show them you truly love them. It is important that we get off the merry-go-round of a hectic world one day a week to reflect on things like *why* we work, *why* we have a family, or *why* we were put in this world. If we don't see the need for this and neglect to reserve this important time for ourselves, we miss out on the richness that a weekly diversion offers. For many of us, it is the only time left in our frenzied modern society that safeguards time for family, self-reflection and meditation.

Make sure that you take at least one day off a week to spend some personal time with your loved ones and to attend to your own personal needs. Even the great religions of the world stress the importance of taking off one day a week for personal time and spiritual reflection. A balanced mind needs not only the satisfaction that comes from productive work but also recreation, stimulation and joy that comes from simple diversions.

How about your vacations? I have often heard managers or executives say something like, "I didn't take a vacation last year" or "I haven't had a vacation in five years." I can assure you that ten or twenty years from now your spouse and children will not be bragging about what a great success you have become. However, what they will remember is that "we never took vacations together as a family." If you have convinced yourself that you are too busy to take a vacation, you frankly are overcompensating your ego. If you have convinced yourself that skipping your vacation will help you to "get ahead" or be recognized by others, stop deluding yourself. If that is what it takes to "get ahead" in your organization, it is time to post your vacation schedule on the employee bulletin board. Then begin to look for another job where one's skills and talents are appreciated more than how many hours they log in. A vacation is important. You have earned it, you need it, demand it and take your vacation time.

A few years ago I saw a television biography of John Adams, an early American president, on television. I am sure it was fictionalized as they showed his family gathered around the old man in his final moments. In this television drama, some of the final words of the ancient patriot rang out loud and clear. As he went in and out of consciousness he shouted, "WORK!" "WORK!" The intent of this scene was to show the deep Puritan roots that were embedded in Adam's character and how the concept of hard work permeated his entire life. As I watched this I thought, "How sad. There were so many *better* things to say or think at the time." Work is important, and it should be rewarding and fulfilling, but it shouldn't be the most important thing in life. Work is also not a substitute for meaningful relationships. This leads us to the next chapter and principle.

Recap of Principle #8

Take the time right now to examine your life. Make sure you are achieving a work/life balance by choosing to *reserve* time for your simple diversions. This important step will help you reach your full potential. These diversions should be enjoyed daily, weekly, and annually. Furthermore, they should be considered as important as any other thing you do. Find a distraction from the daily routine that you really enjoy, and make it your own special pursuit.

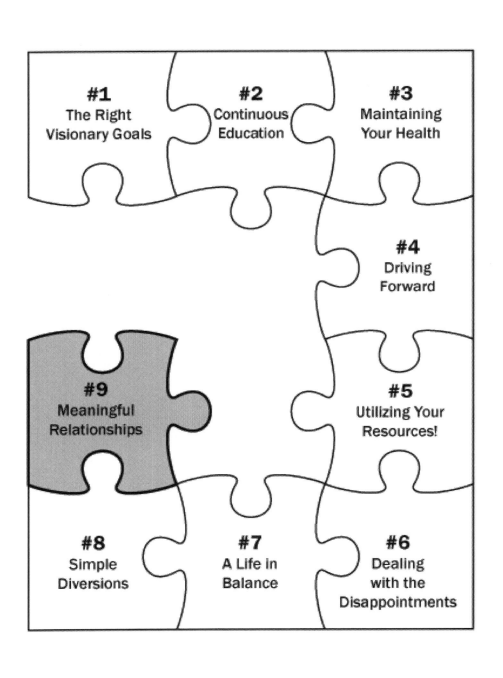

PRINCIPLE #9

MEANINGFUL RELATIONSHIPS

Jean Paul Getty was an American industrialist and the billionaire founder of the Getty Oil Company. He inherited a fortune from his father who was in the petroleum business, but he was also a successful businessman in his own right. He lived the latter part of his life in England and struggled with finding personal fulfillment. Married five times, he was once quoted as saying, "A lasting relationship with a woman is only possible if you are a business failure." He was also later to remark that he would trade all his wealth for *one* happy marriage. How important is having a *meaningful relationship* in life? It is so important that literally every human culture on earth is centered on this universal need. Humankind has created thousands of poems, love stories, movies, songs, and even great buildings (like the Taj Mahal) to express the need for a meaningful relationship with another person. Yet, for many, enjoying a loving bond with another person seems to be an elusive dream that partly consumes their energy as they stumble from one unhappy relationship to another.

I have been very fortunate and blessed in life. My wife BJ and I first met in 1971. We were married three years later and had three wonderful daughters. As a family, we have had our good times and challenging times, but mostly they have been very good. We are certainly not perfect, but we appreciate the relationships we all have with one another. Our children did not experience seeing their parents shouting or fighting with each other. BJ and I did not allow a family culture of name calling and finger pointing because we treasured our special relationship. Today, we also have grandchildren and sons-in-law, and we have tried hard to include them in what we believe is a positive, caring family culture.

Our Need For Meaningful Relationships

From the moment of birth, we are intended to be creatures that need and value loving relationships. Unless prohibited by accident or unfortunate circumstances, we are nurtured by a loving mother who teaches us of the need for bonding and affection. If we are blessed, we also have a loving father who models valuable masculine characteristics like strength, kindness and integrity for us to observe. As we go through life, we have exceptional opportunities to develop and maintain meaningful relationships.

What do I mean when I use the term *meaningful relationship*? First, I mean a loving emotional connection of bonding between two people that provides affection and delight. This interrelationship is something special because it adds an additional dimension to life, including a deeper purpose and a *sharing* that we can't receive through acquaintances or associates. Secondly, these relationships may be between parent and child, siblings, spouses, distant relatives, or just very close friends.

But I must offer a word of caution. Some relationships are *toxic* and should never be established in the first place. Other potential relationships should be avoided because of the harm they will create, especially if you have *different* value systems. We should be kind and friendly with everyone, but before we invest the time and emotional energy to take friendship to the next level of a meaningful relationship, we should consider the consequences involved. I have known some fine people who were taken down the path of drug abuse, financial ruin, and serious emotional trauma because they formed a toxic relationship with another person. Not every friend or personal acquaintance we are *attracted* to should be embraced in a deeper relationship simply because of convenience or opportunity. Remember, life is full of choices; so please choose wisely.

So why are meaningful relationships so important? They allow us to have an emotional connection that is uniquely human. Caring relationships provide an elevated feeling of purpose as we do rewarding things *with* and *for* someone we love. These are the kinds of rewarding relationships where we can be real and candid, confidentially communicating our deepest thoughts, hopes, or frustrations. We can have complete trust and allow ourselves to be vulnerable without fear of humiliation or betrayal. We can have an *intimate* bond with another that fills a natural and healthy longing we have had since birth. It is in this kind of a relationship we can feel comfortable laughing, crying, rejoicing, and mourning together. It provides a level of contentment, oneness, and sheer pleasure we can't find anywhere else or in any other way.

How are your relationships? Are they truly meaningful or just superficial? Are there relationships that need to be mended or strengthened that you have avoided or are taking for granted? Make an effort to strengthen these relationships now. As I have stated in an earlier principle, don't allow time to make these decisions for you or limit your options. You probably won't like the decision that it makes. There is no better time for you to begin to mend meaningful relationships than *right now*!

I am reminded of a story about a husband and wife who were giving each other the "silent treatment" by refusing to talk to one another. The husband was a business man and needed to leave on an important trip the next morning.

He wrote a note to his wife and left it on her pillow, and it said, "Wake me up at 5:00 A.M. tomorrow morning." The next morning he woke up and looked at the clock and it was 8:00 A.M. The husband was furious that he missed his airline flight, but his wife was already awake and out of the room. Just then he noticed a little note by his pillow.

It said, "Wake UP.—it's 5:00 A.M."

Why should we mend a hurting relationship? We just simply assume that there will be many tomorrows. We sometimes act as if we are *entitled* to a long life, as if it is owed to us. This is a false assumption because no one has been given the promise of another tomorrow in this world. In Western society we don't even like to discuss death. We want to mask its reality with words like "passed" or "departed" or "no longer with us." We sanitize the prospect of death by sending many of the dying to hospitals, and we use modern embalming methods to make the dead seem like they are *still* alive, only sleeping. But the harsh reality is that life is short, and *if* we receive the gift of another day, only then, will we be here tomorrow. Everyday is a precious endowment, and each morning, as the first waking consciousness of a new day enters our minds, we should be thankful for the gift of another day of life.

This means that we need to allow others the room to make some mistakes. No one is perfect, and even those who love us deeply will occasionally be insensitive and disappoint us. It is important for us to have a balanced and mature expectation of our relationships. They may have a few habits or personality quirks that bother us. But the great benefits of their love far outweigh the small things that may irritate us. Maturity means that we learn to focus on and appreciate the good things we love about that person. We should give them the right to be human and have faults. If they can't change or are unwilling to modify their behaviors, we must change how we deal with or react to their imperfections. Think of the dozens of good qualities they have rather than their faults and idiosyncrasies. Immature people focus on the annoyances of others, and in time these seeds grow into reasons for conflict. Just like our loved ones have faults, we *also* have faults. Just like those we love may irritate us, we also irritate others. What is important is that we choose to focus on their positive traits and not on their weaknesses.

The Law of Cause and Effect

The study of science reveals that the law of "cause and effect" is active throughout the universe, and that includes events in our lives. What we are tomorrow is determined by the choices we make today. Just like the present has roots to our past, the future has roots in the present. This law called *cause and effect* is neutral and of itself is neither bad nor good. If we sow bad seeds, we will eventually reap a bad harvest. Yet, if we sow good seeds, we will eventually enjoy the positive benefits of a good harvest. It is important to remember that life does have a sort of "layaway plan." Someday the decisions we make (or refuse to make) will come to harvest. In fact, even indecision over time becomes a way to make a decision. We either *choose* to decide and control our own options, or time will make the decision for us. For a person interested in his or her own personal leadership, to live is to choose.

So what are some of the attitudes or actions that get in the way of having meaningful relationships with others, including our parents, children, spouse, friends, and distant relationships?

Traits That Harm Relationships

Let's look at some traits that are guaranteed to eventually harm or *destroy* virtually any possibility of affection or bonding between two people.

Selfishness is a serious personal problem that can destroy any relationship. This selfishness may be either on our part or the part of another. It destroys trust and erodes the emotional glue that bonds people together. The reason is that being selfish is not concerned with the needs and wants of both parties; it is only concerned with "me" twenty-four hours a day, seven days a week. Even when a selfish person outwardly does something good or kind for another person, there is usually a *hidden agenda* beneath the action. On the other hand, trying to please a selfish person is frustrating. No matter what you do, it is never enough, and what you have done is soon forgotten. Selfishness is a toxin that will poison any relationship.

Familiarity or taking a person for granted is another problem that can kill a relationship. This becomes a challenge in many marriages. It is easy to just assume that a loved one will be nearby forever. They may even appear to be outwardly content. This is a dangerous attitude because all good relationships must be nurtured and cultivated to become or remain healthy. If you plant a nice garden of vegetables or flowers but don't nurture or cultivate the garden, it will eventually become overrun with *other* things. The plants may grow for a while, but they will be stunted. Eventually, they will become overwhelmed and shadowed by larger and more aggressive plants. The same is true of our personal relationships. They also need time, love, and care. Without nurturing and appreciation, any bond between two people will become overshadowed by allegedly bigger issues. Eventually, taking a relationship for granted tells the other person you really don't care about them like you once did.

Insecurity and fear is a common problem in many relationships. This is where one individual has a personal problem with trust or commitment, usually due to a past traumatic experience. This individual has trouble communicating and sharing because they don't want to be *vulnerable* to another person, even someone they love. In time, this can wound a relationship because the other person wants and needs someone they *can* communicate with. This lack of trust and sharing eventually makes the relationship unfulfilling. The incompatibility of each other's needs and level of commitment will ultimately harm the relationship.

Chronic jerkism is a catch-all phrase I use to describe an attitude that some have which leads them to believe they must *always* be right, always argue, and always have the last word. Frankly, this is a severe personality dysfunction that repels people. It is typically caused by insecurity and a lack of self-worth, and it incites an individual to constantly want to *prove* how right they are. This is a frustrating person to have a relationship with, and eventually he or she will become noxious to those who are exposed to this attitude for an extended period of time.

Maintaining Positive Relationships

So how do we establish and maintain positive and meaningful relationships?

One way we establish or grow a meaningful relationship is to *invest* in that relationship. If I were to be given a large amount of money, and I wanted it to *grow* and increase in value, I would need to invest that money. To increase this investment would require my time, attention, and patience to ensure long-term growth. In a similar way, a meaningful relationship requires spending time with others. We must invest our full attention, personal concern, and loving patience to maintain the relationship even with obstacles like distance or a difference of opinion on certain issues.

Years ago, I remember a college chancellor remarking in a forum that there are basically *two* ways of life. One is the "way of give" and the other is the "way of get." To have a satisfying relationship with another person requires practicing the *way of give*. Every aspect of a healthy bond between two people is about giving. When you sit and listen to someone, you are *giving* of your time. When your advice is solicited and you provide it, you are *giving* of your knowledge and wisdom. When you do enjoyable things together and laugh, play, or cry, you are *giving* your intimacy. When you buy dinner or give someone a gift, you are *giving* of your financial resources. If both individuals in a relationship are "givers," it is a priceless relationship that can't be beat.

However, what if *you* are a giver but others you love and have meaningful relationships with are not givers? Perhaps they are not entirely selfish, but they don't seem to have the same desire to give to the relationship as you do? The first thing I suggest is to *lead* by example. Like most things in life, a balance is required here. Take an interest in their life and discover a specific area where you share a strong interest. Then offer to help in a small but significant way that shows you have a genuine concern for what is going on in their life. Don't make the mistake of immediately giving too much, or you may actually harm the relationship. You don't want to create a dependency or an obligation of debt on their part toward you. This can lead to resentment and the *appearance* that you are doing these things to manipulate or control them. Let them know you care for them and want to help them in reasonable ways. Occasionally ask, "What can I do to help?" Eventually, this person will recognize your kindness and consideration and will begin to respond in a similar way toward you if they esteem your love and friendship. Also, keep in mind that many people are not givers because they don't feel like they have anything to give. Perhaps they have been wounded in the past by people they loved or trusted, or perhaps they lack the resources to feel like they can give very much. Be a mature person and willingly give without expectation that you will immediately receive something in return.

Healing a Damaged Relationship

What if you are trying to heal damaged relationships that are hurting? Nothing is as effective as a heartfelt apology and a sincere admission of error. You might start by sending a card. Be specific about what you did wrong and ask for their forgiveness. Do not negate this effort by pointing out or mentioning something they did wrong. Do not use something they said, or did as an excuse for why you did something wrong. Only they can come to see their own error and eventually respond back to you in a similar manner. After sending the card, allow a little time and ask them out to a meal at a public restaurant. Again, apologize to them and candidly acknowledge the things you did that were wrong. Expect the other person to "vent" or show anger toward you. Allow them to "let off steam" and release thoughts they have probably been containing for a long time. Don't cut them off or attempt to correct them. Listen intently and take responsibility for your *own* actions. Offer no excuses or scapegoating of others. Do your part and personally ask for forgiveness. If you did something serious, or have done something repeatedly, I encourage you to get professional help. If this is the case, let them know you are taking responsibility and "ownership" of your problem and are getting professional help. The rest is up to them, and depends on their level of commitment to the relationship. Hopefully they will respond with a desire for reconciliation. If not, at least you did the right thing, and in time they may come to see their need to apologize for their actions and reach out to you.

Why is all of this important? It is because truly *meaningful* relationships are the most gratifying and pleasurable parts of life. Other things may come and go including money, prestige, titles, or power. Yet, to possess these things without meaningful relationships still results in a feeling of emptiness or incompleteness in life. This is so true that wealthy or powerful individuals are willing to spend large amounts of money or risk their reputations just to discover even *one* meaningful relationship that will make them truly happy. If necessary, they are willing to buy love or sex as a poor temporary substitute for a relationship that could provide them with real intimacy and fulfillment. On the other hand, I have known people who maintained wonderful personal relationships. Due to circumstances they lost their money, titles, and health. But what sustained them and gave them the *greatest* satisfaction were the personal relationships they came to value and treasure.

Recap of Principle #9

In conclusion, let your *loved* ones know everyday just how *special* they are. You may not get another chance in this lifetime. Too many people *delay* spending time with their loved ones, thinking they can do it on vacation, or in retirement, or during the holidays. Like the need for personal growth, it is often put off until it is too late. This is especially important if you have parents, grandparents, aunts, uncles, or elderly friends and relatives. Talk to them today, because each day is a gift. If you have a poor relationship with someone with whom you should have a special bond, make a serious effort to heal the breach and rebuild a new relationship.

Remember, *people* are more important than possessions.

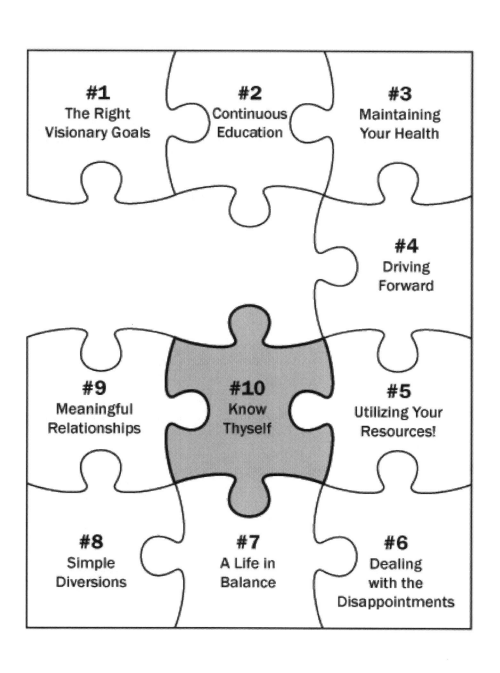

PRINCIPLE #10

KNOW THYSELF

An ancient religious text states, "The human mind is the most deceitful of all things. No one can understand how deceitful it is." Within each of us lies a tremendous power that has the ability to produce great good or abundant evil. We are all capable of either or both of these traits, and if you look at the history of humankind's many leaders, this becomes evident. Some historical leaders were caring and generous people. They gave of themselves to serve, nurture, and mentor others. It was their goal to lift up certain groups or nations to become better and more prosperous. Yet, other historical rulers have been the exact opposite. They were hard and selfish people. They ruthlessly took what they could from others. It was their goal to seize everything they could from certain groups or nations, often including their own. They greedily desired to control others without caring what would happen to them. To these destructive rulers, people were simply something to be used for their personal gain. Abraham Lincoln once stated, "Nearly all men can stand adversity, but if you want to test a man's character, give him power."

Most historical leaders have possessed a *mixture* of good and bad qualities. We are reminded in the biblical creation story that the first man and woman took fruit from the tree of the *knowledge* of good and evil. This symbolically means that the entire human race, including us, is a blended mixture of "good and evil" thoughts, attitudes, and motives. However, one side of this mixture usually controls and dominates the other.

Knowing Your Own Heart

How well do you know your own heart, and what are you capable of doing? In ancient Greece, the aphorism "know yourself" was inscribed in the forecourt of the temple of Apollo at Delphi. This succinct statement should arouse us to think about the human nature we struggle with on a daily basis. As just mentioned, this human nature is a *mixture* of good and evil. It influences our own morals, judgments, temperament, habits, and abilities to control ourselves when necessary. Let's begin to examine some important ways we can begin to *know thyself.*

First, how well do you take criticism or correction? Most of us bristle when we are criticized by others. Our natural reaction is, "Who do you think you are?" Often, we respond by looking for *faults* in our accuser to neutralize what has been said about us. But a better and more honest approach was demonstrated by the example of U.S. President Abraham Lincoln. One of the prominent members of Lincoln's cabinet was a talented man named Edwin Stanton. As Lincoln's Secretary of War, he shared the daily burdens of conducting the American Civil War with the President. One day he became very frustrated with Lincoln, and others heard him call Lincoln a "fool." Of course, this comment got back to Lincoln, and his response tells us a lot about his character. He replied, "Well, Stanton is a wise man, and if he called me a fool, I had better look into it." I thought of this story recently when I saw a highly successful televangelist interviewed on national television. Joel Osteen leads a mega church in Houston, Texas. He was asked pointedly how he responds to personal criticism about the focus of his preaching. The question was asked by the reporter in an accusatory tone that bordered on being rude. His reply was, "The first thing I do is look at *myself* and see if it is true, or if I am doing something to give that impression."

The way to make harsh judgment serve a good purpose is to be humble enough to learn from it. It is a great person indeed who searches through even the most severe criticism to discover *any* element of truth. In contrast, most people simply dismiss anything they hear that is unpleasant or immediately become defensive with counter-charges of criticism. However, we need to *know thyself* enough to not only recognize our faults and weaknesses but also the impression we leave with other people. There is a common saying today that *perception is reality*. For example, if we have a negative habit or a personality trait that gives the impression of us being selfish or arrogant or uncaring, we need to be aware of it. Once we are aware of this impression, we can do things to soften that image. We can't easily change our personality, but perhaps we can smile more, ask people more questions to show we are interested in them, or make a greater effort to *help* others when we see a genuine need.

Like many things, listening to criticism requires poise. Some individuals will criticize you for the simple reason that they are jealous of you. We must be open-minded enough to accept criticism and learn from it, but we must never allow our critics to stop us from pursuing a worthy goal. We can often learn more about ourselves from our enemies than we do our friends, but we should always hold on to a matter of *conscience* when challenged. Criticism should be viewed as a legitimate reason to pause, reflect, and discover how we can become better than we are. This opportunity for personal growth should be welcomed, but it should never cause us to abandon a beneficial goal or mission. Virtually all of the great leaders in human history had personal problems and flaws. If people waited for *perfection* to lead or follow others, we would still be living in the Stone Age. Never allow criticism or a personal flaw to stop you from achieving something great.

A few years ago, I read an interesting story about Dr. Martin Luther King. He was reputedly addressing a religious congregation about the need for their support of civil rights activism in their own community. Many members of the audience had serious concerns and expressed why they should *not* get involved. One individual stated, "We may be recognized and lose our jobs." Another commented, "Police may become violent and we may get hurt." Others in the audience also passionately expressed reasons why getting involved might result in pain, physical abuse, or even possible death. After listening to these concerns for a while and attempting to respond to them as they arose, Dr. King was seemingly exasperated with some in the audience. Then he loudly proclaimed, "If we are not willing to die for *something*, we are not *fit* to live." By his own personal example, Martin Luther King was willing to die for the principles he believed in, and he did. Do you *know thyself* well enough to be willing to sacrifice your wealth, career, or even your life for a worthy mission? After all, we ask our military personnel who protect us to do this everyday.

What Are You Willing to Live For?

Thankfully, personal leaders are seldom required or asked to literally die for the causes we believe in or the changes we desire to see. Outside of the military, leaders are rarely expected to make the ultimate sacrifice. So for most of us, the real question we need to ask ourselves is, "What am I willing to live for?" Values worth dying for are also worth living for. Many years ago I watched an old Hollywood movie that reenacted the events of the American Civil War. In one scene, President Lincoln called a young man into his office to discuss his enlistment in the intelligence efforts of the Union Army. Lincoln was probing the man to see if he had the qualities to become a good spy.

As the men were talking, Lincoln asked him, "Jim, how much do you love your country?" Jim responded by saying, "Mr. President, I reckon I would be willing to die for her." Lincoln promptly replied, "Jim, I can find 10,000 men who are willing to *die* for the Union. I want you to *live* for her!"

Have you taken the time to determine just what things are worth living for? Do you *know thyself* enough to easily explain them to others without hesitation? Do they inspire you and add a sense of purpose to your life? One of the items at the very top of your list should be the value of integrity. What are you willing to personally *sacrifice* in order to maintain your integrity and not "sell out" when pressure is put on you to conform to other people or groups?

No amount of worldly possessions, including wealth, fame, or power, is a substitute for integrity. Why is integrity so important? The answer is rather simple. Wealth, fame, and power are fleeting and typically unfulfilling. Once attained, or even partially attained, the need is for *more and more* to satisfy. Meanwhile, if one has sacrificed his or her integrity to achieve these things, eventually the only thing remaining is the dishonor of compromise and nothing of lasting value.

In contrast, those who live by the principles that they know are honorable and right live with integrity. They remain content and fulfilled regardless of their financial or social circumstances. Their greatest possessions are inner peace, personal contentment, and self-respect. Their integrity influences and inspires people around them, and this will continue for many generations to come. They leave a legacy of genuineness behind them and in front of them. Just think of the two examples I have mentioned in this chapter. Neither Lincoln nor Dr. King acquired great wealth in their lifetimes, and both probably had more people who despised them than admired them in their lifetimes. They both had personal flaws and weaknesses. Yet their leadership and integrity has motivated and inspired people for generations. A thousand years from now people will study their lives and continue to admire their commitment to a great cause. They knew where they were grounded. Do you *know thyself*?

I believe this principle is so important that I do a personal self-examination for one entire week every springtime. During this time I also change my eating habits, just to shake things up and get out of my normal pattern. What better time of the year is there to do this than when nature itself is producing new life and energy? I not only look for flaws and weaknesses in my character but also for ways to *reinvent* myself in a new positive direction.

Lessons From the Titanic

What has become known as the *Titanic Disaster* was one of the worst
maritime disasters in history. The British luxury liner named the *Titanic* was
built by the White Star Line and weighed 46,000 gross tons. The ship had been
dubbed *unsinkable* by many experts because of its unique design comprising
of sixteen watertight compartments or bulkheads. It also had a double-walled
steel hull to give it additional protection in case the ship struck another object.
Its maiden voyage in 1912 was to be from Southampton, England to New
York City. On just the fifth day of her maiden journey, around 11:40 PM
on twelfth of April the mighty ship struck an iceberg about ninety-five miles
south of the Grand Banks of Newfoundland.

It was a great tragedy that many historians believe actually accelerated the
decline of the British Empire because of the loss of talented British leaders
from all walks of life who went down on the ship. Of the more than 2220
persons aboard, about 1507 died, including a few American millionaires such
as John Jacob Astor, Benjamin Guggenheim, and Isidor Straus. In spite of
the Titanic being proclaimed unsinkable, the iceberg sufficiently damaged
the ship to make it sink in less than three hours time.

Later investigations found a number of reasons to explain why the disaster
occurred. The ship had been steaming too fast in dangerous, icy waters. The
lifeboat space provided room for only about half of the passengers and crew even
though the *Titanic* had more lifeboats than were required by law at the time.
As water poured into the ship and filled up one of the watertight bulkheads,
it pulled the next bulkhead under the water line, and it also filled. The water
simply cascaded into the next bulkhead, then the next, until the ship filled with
water. A ship named the *Californian* was close to the scene but did not come
to the rescue because its radio operator was off duty and asleep. These are all
valid reasons to explain the extent of the disaster, but they do not explain *why*
the double-walled steel hull failed when the ship hit an iceberg.

The events surrounding the sinking of the *Titanic* have been the subject
of several films and books. However, it was not until September 1985 that
the actual wreck was found resting under about 12,000 feet of water. The
salvage crew was able to bring to the surface some of the steel from the hull
of the ship, and what they have discovered is startling.

Internal Flaws Are Discovered

Recent analysis has revealed that the steel hull of the *Titanic* had a sulfur
content which was too high. A high sulfur content causes steel to become

more brittle as it gets colder. In the icy waters of the North Atlantic, the *Titanic's* hull would break rather than bend if it hit another object. This is exactly what happened. The analysis also showed that the ship had *inferior* rivets that were poorly manufactured even by the standards of the day. The hull of the ship was held together by three million flawed rivets. Surprisingly, the total areas of the holes ripped open by the iceberg were only about the size of a modern refrigerator. Yet whole seams of rivets popped open when it hit the iceberg. A ship that had a mighty and impressive outward appearance was brought down by serious *internal* flaws.

There is a valuable lesson to learn from this example if we are humble enough to take the time to *know thyself.* In life, there will be trials and temptations that test your metal. We also have internal weaknesses that can potentially bring us down. For some, it is a lack of self-discipline or an attraction to destructive things like drugs, promiscuous sex, or toxic relationships. Realize that these kinds of flaws have destroyed millions of people, including some with incredible gifts and potential. Don't let this happen to you. Know who and what you are. Know what your capabilities are and shun the temptations and unsavory areas that will sink your life and bring it down. Especially avoid those enticements to which you are personally *drawn* toward and find most attractive. It only takes one *more* drink to become a drunk driver and end a life. It only takes one accidental drug overdose to kill yourself. It only takes one sexual escapade to acquire a lifelong disease. It only takes one large, foolish purchase to cause severe financial problems.

In the Western world, we use a phrase to describe the weakness in an object. We say there is a "chink in the armor." A chink is a small crack or opening that reveals a weak spot. If one exists in armor plating, it potentially can cause the protection of the armor to fail, exposing the body to physical injury. Yes, you and I also have personal weaknesses that can lead to potential failure if we are not aware of them and do not *guard* against them. Other weaknesses that can lead to problems include unstable emotions, poor attitudes, ignorance, or excessive risk-taking. Narcissism and excessive egos have destroyed many gifted people, including some very powerful leaders, just when they were on the threshold of achieving a great goal.

Lesson From President William Harrison

William Henry Harrison was the ninth president of the United States, and he served in 1841. He was one of the most controversial figures in the early westward expansion of the United States. As a military officer and later as a governor, he took millions of acres of land from Native Americans by military conquest or treaty. He was actually a wealthy planter and slave owner. But in an image cultivated by the marketing professionals of his day, he was elected to the presidency as the legendary *Old Tippecanoe*. He was pictured as a rather *simple* man, a log cabin dweller, and a drinker of hard cider. Of course, this was just political marketing spin, and it was not true.

Interestingly, he was the first president to die *during* his term of office, which lasted exactly one month. Harrison's term was the shortest in U.S. history. What happened to him can teach us valuable lessons about ourselves and risk-taking.

In March of 1841, the 68 year-old President-elect Harrison journeyed to Washington in a triumphal procession. He was seen by many as the hero "Old Tip," as the campaign songs called him. His inauguration address was on March 4, 1841. He wrote his own inaugural address, and because his age had been attacked during the campaign, he felt it necessary to demonstrate his manhood on inauguration day. He gave the longest inaugural address in American history partly because he wanted to debunk campaign accusations that he was too old and unintelligent to be president. His address was almost two hours long, and on a very cold March day, he refused to wear a coat or hat during his speech. He wanted to show himself as a *macho*-man who possessed vitality, vigor, and physical strength. As a result of the frigid temperatures and minimal clothing, he developed a severe cold. It slowly *grew* into pneumonia, and he died only thirty-one days into his presidency.

Again, there is a good lesson to learn from this example if we are humble enough to take the time to *know thyself*. President Harrison thought he had something to prove. He allowed his ego to override common sense, and it cost him his life just when he seemed to have arrived at a great personal goal. His vanity became a *chink in the armor* that brought him down.

Are you motivated to "prove" something to others? I have a friend who spent most of his life trying to "prove" to his father that he had worth. He deeply desired his father's acceptance and affection. Yet, his father never offered acceptance to his dying day. So why do we feel a need to *prove* something to others? Do you *know thyself* deeply enough to understand your own motives? Are you secure in who and what you are without needing to prove it to others?

Are You An Agent of Change?

Another important area worthy of self-examination is how well you adapt to change. Are you an agent of change, or do you fervently resist needed change? In 1991, two German mountain climbers came across a unique discovery in the Tyrolean Alps between Austria and Italy. It had been an unusually warm summer, and the Alpine glacial ice was melting quickly after several years of above-average temperatures. What they found was absolutely incredible. Sticking out of the ice was the 4600-year-old mummified remains of a man who lived in the Neolithic age. The Austrian press quickly dubbed him the "Iceman," and the discovery was a sensational find for science. First of all, his body was very well preserved, including the contents of his last meal. He was clothed in an insulated leather coat and boots. Alongside him was his backpack, a bow, arrows, a copper-headed ax, a flint lighter, and kindling to build a fire. To the complete amazement of researchers, here was a man *frozen in time* for about 4600 years. He was virtually unchanged from the moment he died.

Lesson From the Iceman

There is an analogy I would like to draw from this actual event. How well do you *know thyself* and your capacity to adapt to change? The Iceman died many millennia ago and has not changed. Even though he was in step with *his* times, the world has changed dramatically since the day he was apparently killed by an attacker and frozen in a sudden snowstorm. By modern standards, he has now become an oddity or novelty to study. Many things about him have long ago become obsolete. During the past 4600 years, the world has greatly advanced, but he has not. So there he is, an individual frozen in time, unchanged and now rather primitive. But, if we are not careful, we too can cling to personal habits, ideas, and traits that have become obsolete and well past their time. If we resist learning new things or embracing advancing technology, we will also be past our age. Just like the Iceman, we can become *frozen* in time and greatly limit our potential as a leader of others.

Let's briefly discuss some things that should *never* change. Sound moral principles, ethical judgments, and right values should not change. For example, treating others with respect, dignity, and kindness are universal and timeless principles. Keeping our promises, commitments, and responsibilities are eternal standards. Expressing thankfulness and appreciation to others for the things they do for us or others is a timeless virtue.

Yet, there are certain characteristics and ideas that we need to change in order to achieve our highest potential. Change is not a single accomplishment, but an ongoing project. If we make a serious effort to *know thyself*, we will discover there are many things we possess that have now *outlived* their usefulness. These may include archaic ideas, poor personality traits, negative attitudes, or outmoded work habits. We become so comfortable with these traits we may seldom notice them. But others probably do, and in time they become a barrier to our personal growth and to our ability to lead. Years ago, these traits and ideas may have worked and been effective, but the world has changed with time. When we become primitive and allow our skills to become obsolete, we lose our credibility to lead.

Our Comfort Zone

Personal leadership is not about *comfort zones* or maintaining the status quo; it is about a passion for continual growth and improvement. Every positive and healthy change that has ever occurred in human civilization has only come about by rejecting the way things were as "good enough." Personal leaders accept the challenge to make things better and to inspire others to become better, so everyone can win. In contrast, most people will accept only a very *limited* degree of change or accountability. Therefore, they don't deeply desire to win; they just try not to lose. Political activist and author John Gardner reminds us, "Most people in most organizations most of the time are more stale than they know, more bored than they care to admit. All too often it is because they have not been encouraged to use their own initiative and powers of decision. And if they are not expected to use their decision-making powers, they are off the hook of responsibility." Choosing your own path in life is the opposite of this common workplace dilemma. It is all about initiative, decision-making, and responsibility.

Perform a Regular Self-Appraisal

It is interesting to note that most major religious faiths in the world designate a period of time, or a season, for their followers to perform a candid self-analysis of their lives. A designated time is set aside on the calendar to get to *know* thyself. I encourage you to know your own strengths *and* weaknesses. Work hard to build on your strengths, and use them to propel your life in a positive direction. In addition, work diligently to correct, or at least modify, your weaknesses. A personal leader is willing to do a critical self-appraisal and examination to discover where they *need* to do better. Stephen Covey has written the following powerful statement: "The place to begin building any relationship is inside ourselves, inside our circle of influence, our own character." This inner relationship, like all healthy relationships, must be built around honesty and not self-denial.

Yes, it is indeed important to acknowledge our faults and to accept responsibility for them. However, once this is done, it is also important to let it go and get on with life. We can't change what we did or said yesterday. We can apologize and resolve to be better, but we can't change the past. There is no benefit to mentally "reliving" or beating ourselves up over and over again for something that has already occurred and can't be reversed. We can't do anything about what has *already* happened, but we can learn from it and have a positive effect on tomorrow. This is why you should learn to focus on the present which leads to tomorrow, and not dwell excessively on the past.

Recap of Principle #10

I want to leave you with a final question: why do you *really* want to be a leader? If you desire this primarily to make lots of money, I can guarantee you will end up being incredibly disappointed. While you are consumed with getting all the things that money can buy, you will be losing out on the things money can't buy. Money can't buy respect, honor, contentment, deeply loving relationships, or a purpose that really satisfies. If you desire to lead others primarily for the sake of power or prestige, you will also become greatly disappointed. Like other selfish motives, the craving for power doesn't provide lasting satisfaction.

We are all a mixture of good and evil. It is essential that you honestly and candidly get to *know thyself*. We have obvious flaws and other weaknesses that are not so obvious to us. We also have characteristics that may leave negative perceptions with other people. Only when we take the time to perform a self-examination and analysis can we discover these areas. Personal weaknesses can lead to potential failure if we are not aware of them and guard against them. Especially avoid those enticements to which you are personally *drawn*, and most attracted to. It only takes one serious mistake to bring us down like the *Titanic*. Work hard to build on your strengths, and use them to propel your life in a *positive* direction. In addition, work diligently to correct, root out, or at least modify your weaknesses.

Only when you truly *know thyself* have you discovered your *real* spirit and soul. Remember, the great possessions of life are not simply those things we discover on the outside but also what we discover and develop within ourselves.

PRINCIPLE #11

PASSIONATELY POSITIVE

Many years ago, I heard the story about a father who had two boys. One of his sons was extremely optimistic about life, while the other was very pessimistic. The father wanted to challenge the boys, so he decided to put them into two *different* situations. First, he took his pessimistic son and walked him into a playroom that was encircled with many new gifts. Each one was brightly gift wrapped and had a toy inside. Next, he took his optimistic son and walked him into another playroom that had only two large buckets of horse manure in the center of the room.

The father left the boys alone for awhile and then decided to check on them to see how they were doing in their different environments. As he approached the playroom of his pessimistic son, he noticed it was very quiet. As he opened the door of the playroom, he could see that every new gift was opened and out of the box. Some toys were already broken, and some had not even been used. His father asked him, "Son, how are you doing?" Alone in a corner of the room was his pessimistic son, who uttered with a sad voice, "I am sad and bored."

As the father left this room and approached to see his other son, he heard screaming and howling through the walls. Enthusiastic words like "yippee" and "yahoo" came from this room. As the father opened the door, he noticed that the horse manure was everywhere including all over the walls, ceiling, floor, and even all over his boy. Yet, there was his son beaming with joy in the middle of the room. His father asked him also, "Son, how are you doing?" His son replied, "Great Dad, I'm having lots of fun, and I figure with all the horse poop around here, there's *got* to be a pony somewhere!"

Optimism vs. Pessimism

This story is as good as any *definition* I have ever heard to explain the difference between an optimistic and pessimistic attitude or personality. An optimistic person finds potential and possibility in virtually any situation. On the other hand, a pessimistic person finds scarcity or dissatisfaction in virtually any situation. Which one of these types are you? Earlier, I talked about PMA (positive mental attitude) and how it can affect our health. Now we will discuss how it can affect our overall attitude and general approach toward life.

I first became aware of these differences in people when I was in my early twenties in college. As a *married* student, I was under a lot of stressors that most students didn't experience. I had to not only attend classes and study but also work thirty hours a week and cover the costs of college, a rented home, a car, and utilities. In addition to this, I certainly needed to spend time with my wife and baby daughter. I immediately noticed in the college environment that people reacted differently to the exact *same* circumstances. If the college changed a policy, or rule, it typically affected everyone to about the same degree. Some of my peers reacted like it was just another minor inconvenience while others acted like it was a revolutionary denial of their basic human rights. Some, who were often affected the most by the change, would simply "deal" with it. They would try to find some positive virtues of the new policy. Yet others, who were often the least affected, became bitter and angry.

The human mind is the most powerful tool we possess in this world. How we approach life and its daily problems will absolutely determine our degree of success and personal satisfaction. If you give optimistic people mediocre talents, their positive enthusiasm will make the most of their limited abilities to achieve great things. If you give pessimistic people great talents, their attitude will obstruct their ability to make the most of their talents. More often than not, they will live a life of mediocrity and constant frustration. Negative people focus on the problems of the present, while positive people focus on the great possibilities that always lie ahead.

We draw in toward us those things we constantly think about. It is a contradiction to go through life thinking negative thoughts and expecting good things to happen. Like most things we face in life, we must make a personal choice that no one else can make for us.

Analogy From An Automobile

In my automobile is an automatic transmission lever attached to the steering column. This lever gives me the ability to put the car in forward (low gear) or forward (high gear) or neutral or reverse. It doesn't take any *more* effort for me to put the car in forward-high gear than it does to go backward, but it makes a tremendous difference in the direction I want to go. After I start the car, I have to make the *choice* of which direction I want to head toward.

Regarding my attitude, I face the same choice when I wake up every morning, and so do you. We can choose to live in the past and put our new day on the path of reverse or neutral, or we can choose to go *forward* and make the most of today's opportunities. The reason to do this upon rising in the morning is to set the tone for the entire day. It starts a momentum that will take us in one direction or the other all day long.

What does it mean if we choose to go in *reverse* for the day? This means we will have a pessimistic view of everything and dwell on what we can't do, what we don't have, and why good things never happen to us. It means we find fault in everything and everybody. We will carry baggage from the past with us and have proverbial *chips on our shoulders*. You can't safely drive forward if you are using the rear view mirror for guidance.

What does it mean if we choose to go in *neutral* for the day? This means we don't choose to be optimistic. It means that we start the day undecided as to its outcome, and throughout the day we simply respond to whatever happens.

Yet, when we decide to go forward for the day, a different and powerful perspective takes over. We make a choice to succeed and feel like we can overcome any obstacle. We actually expect good things to happen to us. We begin to see the possibilities in every situation. In essence, we precondition our minds early in the day to glean the most out of life and enjoy the day no matter what challenges or roadblocks arise. So what happens if the day is disappointing and doesn't live up to our expectations? The pessimist says, "I just *knew* this would happen," while the optimist says, "Yes, today was a big challenge with some disappointments, but tomorrow is another day."

Lesson From Henry Ford

When most people hear the name of Henry Ford, they think of a successful man who achieved 161 U.S. patents, founded the Ford Motor Company, and became one of the richest men in America. What you don't often hear about is his previous company named the Detroit Automobile Company. By 1902, he had driven it into bankruptcy because he focused too much on engineering and not enough on marketing. He used this negative experience to learn something positive from a business failure. Henry found more investors and, within a year, began the Ford Motor Company. Actually, there may have been business failures for Henry Ford even before the Detroit Automobile Company. Some researchers believe this history may have been buried after Ford became successful. This kind of failure early in a career would have devastated most people, but not Henry Ford. He was a man with a mission who was positive about his ideas and talents.

Lessons From the Colonel and Others

Another example of someone who saw possibilities in every situation was Colonel Harland Sanders. He was born in 1890, and most of us know him for the business he founded, Kentucky Fried Chicken. Yet the Colonel was not an overnight success, and he was considered by many to be a complete failure when he started the famous chicken business in his senior years. His earlier ventures in life included such jobs as working on a farm, serving in the military, conducting streetcars, being a railroad fireman, serving as a justice of the peace, operating a steamboat ferry, selling insurance and tires, and running service stations. By the age of forty, he began cooking food for travelers who stopped at his service station. His food soon drew greater crowds, and he later opened an actual restaurant to serve food. But that business failed and at age sixty-five he took his $105 Social Security check and started his legendary fried-chicken franchise chain. How internationally famous did this senior citizen become? In a 1976 survey, the Colonel was named the world's *second* most recognizable celebrity.

What was his secret to success? No matter what happened to him, he maintained the drive and positive "can-do" optimism to try yet again to have a breakthrough in life. Rather than wallowing in regret or negativity, he learned from his life experiences and failures while moving forward. Overall, he was known to be an easy-going and personable man, unless you prepared his chicken recipe *incorrectly*. Sanders looked for opportunities in each day. If we look hard enough, we can find positive lessons in virtually any situation.

Those Who Had the "Write Stuff"

Theodor Geisel wrote a unique children's book with an odd style that had not been used before. He received twenty-three *rejections* from publishers, but he was positive his book had merit. Finally, he received an offer from Vanguard Press because an old friend worked at this publisher. His pen name was Dr. Seuss, and he changed children's books forever by writing over sixty books in his career.

It took H. Richard Hornberger seventeen years to write a humorous war story about events in the Korean War. He diligently sent out manuscripts of his work, and it was rejected by twenty-one publishers. But he was *positive* that his own experience at the 8055th Mobile Army Surgical Hospital during the war would be of interest to readers. Finally, it was purchased by the publisher William Morrow. Hornberger used the pseudonym Richard Hooker, and his book entitled *MASH* became a successful movie and television series.

Possessing positive optimism doesn't mean we have to deny the seriousness or gravity of situations or problems. Life is full of challenging and difficult days. The difference is how we personally *interpret* the challenge or difficulty by looking for the good. This principle also affects how we feel physically. A pessimistic attitude can make us feel tired and depleted both physically and emotionally. Sometimes our bodies will not feel energetic or naturally heal themselves until our minds allow it. The powerful connection between mind and body is only now being understood by the medical community.

Example From a Dreamer

In my own life, I can see that positive optimism has served me well. I had many goals as a young adult, and almost all of them have come true. As a young man, I would tell my close friends of all of the goals I had in life. A few years back, one of my close friends "Dave" reminded me that the *only* one I haven't achieved is building a tennis court on my property. There is certainly room for one, but it has become one of those goals that lost value to me as I got older. I am not sure I want to spend my recreation time chasing tennis balls anymore.

In the year 2000, I reached the cap for the maximum amount of earnings subject to Social Security taxes late in the year. This meant that no more Social Security taxes would be taken out of the next couple of pay checks. I took about $500 and founded weLEAD as a nonprofit charitable organization. One person I mentioned this to implied I was a "dreamer" who had little chance of succeeding with only a limited amount of money. I have learned in life that many folks underestimate a positive resolve to set goals and achieve them. Remember what the college registrar wrote to me?

You Can Reprogram Your Thinking

If you have a pessimistic approach to life, you need to reprogram your thinking processes. Being negative and pessimistic is a habit that is developed in childhood or through difficult experiences in life. In time, you have trained your mind to be negative, and you now view the world through a gloomy lens of doubt or wariness. It becomes a conditioned response to whatever happens. Then whenever an unexpected or unusual situation occurs, the mind is immediately flooded with suspicion, cynicism, disapproval, and criticism. However, just as we may have developed habits of pessimism, we can retrain our thoughts and develop new habits of optimism.

I would like to offer just a couple of keys that I believe are the antiserum to the disease of chronic pessimism.

The most effective *medicine* to treat pessimism is sincere gratitude. Gratitude is being thankful to somebody or something for what we possess. When you have gratitude, you don't focus on what you *don't* have; instead you focus on and appreciate what you *do* have. When you do this, life takes on a totally new perspective. You say you have financial troubles? Be glad you live in a nation of plenty where you can rebuild your wealth or start over. Remember the financial problems Henry Ford and Harland Sanders once had? You say you have declining health? Take a walk through a graveyard and you will see that you still have some good time left. You say you are driving an old, unattractive automobile? There are millions of people who have to walk everywhere on foot who would love to have your car. Do you presently have a job you don't like? As you prepare yourself to achieve a better one, remember that there are millions who would like to have *any* job. Plenty of unemployed people would love to receive the salary you do. You say you are not getting along with your spouse? If you don't begin to show more gratitude toward him or her, you may find there are dozens of others who would love to spend their lives with your spouse. As a man once said to me, "When you are contemplating your wife's faults, don't forget that it was those very faults that stopped her from getting a *better* husband!"

Sadly, we often don't truly appreciate people or things until they are gone. Then when they have departed, we wish we had said or done things differently. If we are really grateful for the many things we have in life and show it often, we may avoid behaviors that cause us to lose them.

When you have gratitude, you realize that there are some things in life you can't change. But rather than focus on what's lacking, or who's at fault in these situations, you choose to look for the possibilities in them. Each day you will wake up believing that today is special, and whatever happens, you are going to get the most out of this day.

Beware of Negative Messages

Sustaining a positive approach to daily living also requires a second step. Every day we are bombarded with thousands of messages. In conversation, books, radio, the Internet, newspapers, magazines, billboards and television we are fed a steady diet of what others want us to hear. We are told "buy it now," "warning," "hurry," "try it," "danger," "it's free," and "on sale here." These messages are *competing* for our agreement, money, allegiance, or attention. Most of these messages are designed to *get* something from us and are negative. If we want to improve our attitudes and outlooks on life, we need to turn off many of these messages. We also need to be careful that only ones of value get through to us.

Take a few minutes to read a daily newspaper and you will see my point. Even though few of the events described in the paper will truly affect your life, most articles are negative, discouraging, and irrelevant. Later, after we have forgotten the actual contents of the article, we may wonder why we feel frustrated or discouraged. It is because of what we allowed to enter into our subconscious. The radio is another example. If we are not proactive about want we listen to, we put ourselves at the mercy of the announcer or disk jockey. Will the music they provide be uplifting and encouraging? Or will it be demoralizing and cause anxiety? I am reminded of the story about a person who took a forty-year-old recording of his favorite country music artist and reversed the motor on his old record player so it would play the record backward. When he listened to the country song, the singer got his truck back, his job back, his dog back and his fourth wife *back*.

If you want to be passionately positive, you must learn to turn most of this cultural noise "off." Make a serious effort to control what you listen to and what you allow to enter into your subconscious. Your mind should be like a fertile landscaped garden. If it is neglected, it will be overcome with every type of noxious weed, including faulty, distorted, and discouraging messages. Soon positive thoughts and messages will immediately be choked out by an accumulation of destructive messages. Not actively choosing what you listen to is neglectful, and in time this will produce undesirable results. If you find yourself in this condition, it is time to do some serious self-evaluation. It is time to dig up and uproot the weeds you have been ignoring.

I want to suggest some tips to help you do this. When reading a magazine or newspaper, focus on the articles that really affect you and are not just examples of sensationalism masquerading as journalism. If other articles catch your attention, usually the first paragraph reveals the heart of the story without all the pessimistic details. When watching television, look for programming that makes you feel enlightened or uplifted when the episode ends. The remote's "mute button" is also a great way to avoid listening to the obnoxious commercials that treat you like you have the maturity of a five-year-old child. If you find yourself in a waiting room or lobby, consider bringing your own reading or listening material. Listen to your personal collection of digital audio music or CD's in the car rather than the radio. Remember that Ralph Waldo Emerson once wrote, "A man is what he thinks about all day long."

Recap of Principle #11

We have a choice to make regarding our approach to life and daily problems. Optimism is an attitude and a choice to be positive. It will guide you to look for the best in people and every situation. Optimism will also determine our degree of success and personal satisfaction. In life, we will draw toward us what we constantly think about. Every morning we need to establish a positive attitude and look forward to each day. It is possible to reprogram our thinking by developing sincere gratitude for all the things we have. Taking people or possessions for granted can be costly.

Be selective on what you allow to enter your mind because it will eventually determine what you think and how you feel. If you *cultivate* your mental landscape, you can uproot years of negativity. You can replace what was there with the seeds of new ideas. This will allow you to deepen your convictions and fertilize your creativity. If you water these thoughts with hope and faith, you will eventually achieve a positive outlook that is warmed by the sunlight of satisfaction and peace.

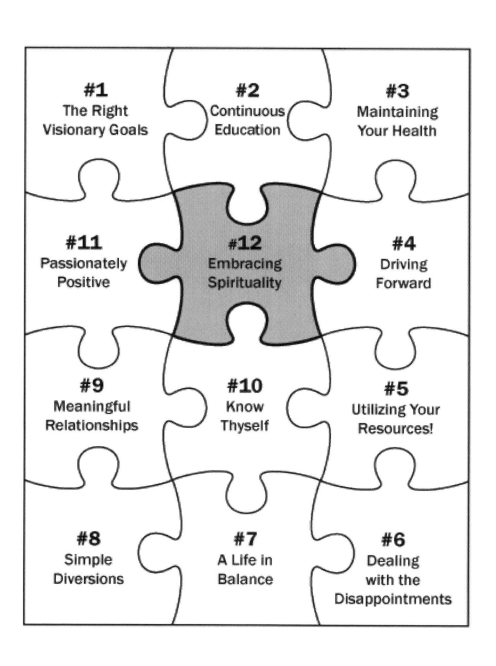

PRINCIPLE #12

<u>EMBRACING SPIRITUALITY</u>

In 2004, former ABC News science correspondent Michael Guillen wrote a thoughtful book entitled *Can a Smart Person Believe In God?* As a theoretical physicist, Guillen offers some insightful comments about the deep importance of spirituality in one's life. He correctly observes that there are two important and distinct qualities about human existence. The first quality is better understood and one about which many people have heard. It is commonly called IQ. This stands for *Intelligence Quotient,* and it refers to our abilities to analyze situations, solve problems and acquire intellectual knowledge. However, there is a second quality that is also extremely important which is lesser known. Sometimes it is blatantly ignored or rejected. It is called SQ. This stands for *Spiritual Quotient,* and refers to our abilities to perceive nonphysical aspects of reality. Possessing both IQ and SQ gives one the enhanced ability to solve complex physical and nonphysical problems through spiritual knowledge and conviction. Our journeys through life are maximized when we fervently seek both a higher level of IQ and SQ.

Allow me to provide an analogy. Our vision works best when we have two healthy eyes. Even though they are positioned differently in the head, both eyes combined are able to see in stereo and balance different dimensions by focusing together. There is more to dimension and reality than can be seen by just one eye. In a process called *stereopsis*, the human brain pools the two flat one-dimensional images from each eye and converges these images together to create a stereoscopic image.

In a similar way, there is more to perceive about our existence than can be attained by simply possessing a high IQ. This is especially true if we neglect or deny our need for SQ. If we ignore our SQ, we are looking at the purpose and reality of human life from a limited, single perspective and dimension!

Guillen also writes that someone who embraces physical science and denies spirituality is an Intellectual Cyclops. On the other hand, a religious person who embraces theology but denies scientific discovery is a Spiritual Cyclops. Ralph Waldo Emerson once said, "The religion that is afraid of science dishonors God and commits suicide." Some insist that science and religion are at odds. This is not necessarily so. What is usually at odds are different people's personal interpretations of science or religion.

Religion in History

So what has religious belief done for the world? The critics of spirituality are the first to point out that more wars have been fought over religion than any other cause in human history. What this tells us is that people get passionate about their religious beliefs in the same way they become passionate about allegiances to their families or their nations. Passion can be an emotion used for good or evil. The recent twentieth century recorded the bloodiest wars in human history, and it included two great world wars. However, they were not fought over religious issues, but they were spawned by *secular* rulers or movements dedicated to nationalism or fascism.

The truth is that many of civilization's greatest achievements and advances were also a result of passionate people of religious faith. We have established our greatest educational institutions, achieved significant scientific breakthroughs, cured diseases, comforted the afflicted, and advanced civil freedom primarily due to deeply religious individuals. In 2002, the *NonProfit Times* reported on the seven largest publically supported philanthropies in the United States. Each one had religious origins and had been founded by individuals who possessed a strong spiritual faith.

Other critics of spirituality boldly proclaim that religion is simply a myth needed to comfort the superstitious or ignorant. The truth is that history is documented with the lives of people who achieved great things because their faith led them to believe in something bigger than themselves. In spite of opposition, their spirituality motivated them to continue when *others* decided to stop and give up.

Most personal leaders realize and accept the fact that there is indeed a *spiritual element* to life. They may not totally understand it, or always sense it, but they know it is there. I realize the discussion of spirituality is not considered vogue or "politically correct" in many circles today. It is for this reason that I have saved this important principle for last. If I had placed it first, I believe some readers of the book would have never gotten beyond the first principle. That attitude is to their personal detriment. Respected author and management consultant Peter Block reminds us, "Spirituality is the process of living out a set of deeply held personal values, of honoring forces or a presence greater than ourselves. It expresses our desire to find meaning in, and to treat as an offering, what we do."

This spiritual element provides a number of positive characteristics that cannot be found or nurtured anywhere else. Personal leaders know the purpose of their existence must go far beyond the pursuit of the "whoever dies with the most toys wins" philosophy of our modern society. They know that every day of life is a precious gift and an endowment to become something or someone even better. This spiritual element also provides them a mental toughness to endure the difficult periods of their lives. They come to realize that sad or tragic things also happen for a *purpose,* even if we do not yet understand exactly what the reason is. There are a few moments in United States history that highlight this fact. An example is the *Declaration of Independence* written in 1776. But before we discuss its content, let's remember the times in which it was written.

The Spirit of '76

For over one thousand years the Western world believed in the *divine right of kings.* This political and religious philosophy taught that all kings and queens ruled under the direct authority of God. They were ordained and given their royal titles and offices by the direct will of God. Any challenge to their rule was not only rebellion against the civil authority but also rebellion against the will of the Creator. This concept was supported by the interpretation of the evangelist Paul in the New Testament book of Romans when he wrote in Chapter 13 that "every soul should be subject to the governing authorities. For there is no authority except from God, and the authorities that exist are appointed by God. Therefore whoever resists the authority resists the ordinance of God, and those who resist will bring judgment on themselves."

The North American group of British citizens who fostered civil rebellion and a declaration of independence were well aware of these traditional and entrenched beliefs. There were many Protestant ministers who preached the need to be in subjection to the existing civil authorities. So by what authority could they rebel against the British crown? The answer is revealed in the Declaration of Independence as modified and ratified by the second Continental Congress of 1776. In a bold demonstration of *underlying* spirituality, this document acknowledged the presence of God three times in its text. The divine providence of God was used as a reason and justification for rebellion from the British crown. Here are the *three* references in bold type:

> When in the Course of human events, it becomes necessary for one people to dissolve the political bands which have connected them with another, and to assume among the Powers of the earth, the separate and equal station to which the Laws of Nature and of **Nature's God** entitle them, a decent respect to the opinions of mankind requires that they should declare the causes which impel them to the separation.

> We, therefore, the Representatives of the United States of America, in General Congress, Assembled, appealing to the **Supreme Judge** of the world for the rectitude of our intentions, do, in the Name, and by Authority of the good People of these Colonies, solemnly publish and declare, That these United Colonies are, and of Right ought to be Free and Independent States.

> And for the support of this Declaration, with a firm reliance on the Protection of **Divine Providenc**e, we mutually pledge to each other our Lives, our Fortunes and our sacred Honor.

Was the Revolution a Death Wish?

Let's remember what signing this document actually meant to the signatories. It was a *suicide pact* for these fifty-six men to write their names to a document that would be considered treasonous. They were challenging the greatest military power on earth, and they were surrounded by many neighbors who were still loyal to the British crown. The odds of achieving independence were slim. The odds of being captured and hung for treason were great. So what drove them to sign the document? By what authority could these individuals declare independence and violate the established divine right of kings? They tell us that Nature's God entitled them, that the Supreme Judge of the World would judge their intentions, and that they would rely on Divine Providence for protection and success.

The *Declaration of Independence* was greatly influenced by Enlightenment thinkers who believed that government existed by consent of the governed and that people should rebel if their natural rights, granted by the Creator, were violated. Furthermore, they concluded that all men are created equal and possess certain inalienable rights provided by Nature's God.

Actually, in Jefferson's original draft, he also used the phrase "we hold these truths to be sacred," but it was modified to "we hold these truths to be self-evident" to avoid having the document sound like a sermon. What drove them to suffer harassment, potential loss of material possessions, and possible death? It was a belief that what they were doing mattered for *future* generations because they were part of a movement approved by Divine Providence. It was the spirituality possessed by many of the delegates that drove them to the greatest level of commitment and service when reality told them to stop and go home.

How about your life and personal goals? Do you have the benefit of spirituality to guide and inspire you when everything seems lost? Do you have both a high IQ and SQ?

Another example of how spirituality provides mental toughness is recorded in the notes of the Constitutional Convention of 1787. After the United States achieved independence, the nation struggled because it had a weak central government. The existing *Articles of Confederation* insured the strong independence of each state but the weakness of the central government. The quarrels between the states were deep and divisive. There was no real *union* of the colonies at this time. Each state raised or lowered tariffs on goods from others, and some minted their own money. The northern states insisted that political representation be based on population while the southern states claimed representation should be based upon land under cultivation. The smaller states feared they would be overwhelmed and controlled by the large states. And the topic of slavery simmered over every major issue between the northern and southern states. Almost all the states were concerned that a strong federal government would interfere in their own affairs. The leaders of the nation recognized this fact and gathered together to find a solution. It was a sweltering hot summer day in Philadelphia as about thirty delegates from twelve of the thirteen states met in a small room at the State House in Philadelphia during this historic constitutional convention.

The delegates had been arguing for over four weeks, and the convention was about to disband in failure. Actually, it would come to the brink of collapse many times. History records that the personality of General George Washington was perhaps the only unifying force. These former colonies had come only so far in the eleven years since 1776, and the disunited states were on the verge of collapse. In the midst of this very convention, it seemed that all the events leading to independence and freedom may have been in vain.

On the 28ᵗʰ of June, at one of the most critical times during this convention, its most elderly statesman rose to speak.

Have We Forgotten That Powerful Friend?

Next to George Washington, this talented 81-year-old man was one of the most respected and revered patriarchs of the original American revolution. He simply asked the president of the convention if he could address the delegates. His request was granted, and at this critical moment he rose and spoke quietly. It was none other than Dr. Benjamin Franklin, the aged patriot, who spoke to the divided delegates. Here is what he said:

> Mr. President
>
> The small Progress we have made, after 4 or 5 weeks close Attendance and continual reasonings with each other, our different Sentiments on almost every Question, several of the last producing as many "Noes" as "Ayes," is, methinks, a melancholy Proof of the Imperfection of the Human Understanding.
>
> In this Situation of this Assembly, groping, as it were, in the dark to find Political Truth, and scarce able to distinguish it when presented to us, how has it happened, Sir, that we have not hitherto once thought of humbly applying to the Father of Lights to illuminate our Understandings? In the Beginning of the Contest with Britain, when we were sensible of Danger, we had daily Prayers in this Room for the Divine Protection. Our Prayers, Sir, were heard;—and they were graciously answered. All of us, who were engaged in the Struggle, must have observed frequent Instances of a superintending Providence in our Favor. To that kind Providence we owe this happy Opportunity of Consulting in Peace on the Means of establishing our future national Felicity. And have we now forgotten that powerful Friend? or do we imagine we no longer need its assistance?
>
> I have lived, Sir, a long time; and the longer I live, the more convincing proofs I see of this Truth—that God governs in the Affairs of Men. And if a Sparrow cannot fall to the Ground without his Notice, is it probable that an Empire can rise without his Aid? We have been assured, Sir, in the Sacred Writings, that "except the Lord build the House, they labour in vain that build it." I firmly believe this; and I also believe, that, without his concurring Aid, we

shall succeed in this political Building no better than the Builders of Babel; we shall be divided by our little, partial, local Interests, our Projects will be confounded, and we ourselves shall become a Reproach and a Bye-word down to future Ages. And, what is worse, Mankind may hereafter, from this unfortunate Instance, despair of establishing Government by human Wisdom, and leave it to Chance, War, and Conquest.

I therefore beg leave to move—that henceforth Prayers, imploring the Assistance of Heaven and its Blessing on our Deliberations, be held in this Assembly every morning before we proceed to Business; and that one or more of the Clergy of this city be requested to officiate in that Service.

Except for three or four persons, the majority of delegates thought prayers were unnecessary and defeated the resolution. However, the convention rested for a day, and many of the delegates sought God's guidance through private personal prayer and fasting. The convention then reconvened, and eventually a constitution was approved. Franklin's stirring reminder of *spirituality* and what was at stake for future generations resulted in a breakthrough that made the Constitution possible. It was not a perfect charter, and almost immediately it needed amendments. Yet, it was an appeal to their spirituality that prompted many delegates to submerge their petty differences and craft a basic constitution that forever changed the world and how people are governed. It has endured with amendments for over two hundred years and has become the democratic template used to introduce freedom to many other nations.

Many are Embarrassed By Spirituality

If you think about it, we still face the same problem that Franklin faced with most of the delegates. Many people are uncomfortable hearing about the topic of spirituality. Can you imagine sitting in a large publicly owned corporation and discussing a very complex and convoluted problem? Perhaps a large loan is being contemplated or massive layoffs of employees are anticipated. Maybe a merger is being discussed or bankruptcy is looming if things don't change. Now picture a senior executive of the corporation standing up and suggesting that the executive team have a prayer to seek Divine guidance on their serious decision. What do you think the reaction would be? Some would be obviously embarrassed by the suggestion, others might be offended, and a few would be in shock that a suggestion of this type was even presented. This is why your own *personal* embrace of spirituality is so important. You may not be able to influence a group or committee to realize that IQ and SQ are essential to sound decision-making, but *you can* make the choice on your own. In the privacy of your own home and thoughts, you can seek Divine favor and guidance. I am pleased to say that I do sit on the board of directors of a small company, and every board meeting *does* begin with a prayer for guidance and wisdom.

Jefferson and Franklin understood that what we do, or don't do, has consequences far beyond today and the present generation. Both of these patriots rejected the traditional religious institutions of their day and held rather quirky personal beliefs. Yet, they were guided by their Spiritual Quotient and realized that we will all stand in a *higher* court than any physical one where we are judged today. It is the final verdict in that higher court that will really count.

There is one definite thing that believers in God and atheists have in common. They both believe in something they can't prove by scientific methods. People who believe in God have *faith* in a higher power, and atheists have faith in randomness. One belief system inspires individuals to attain phenomenal achievements while personally facing depravation, pain, or death. The other belief system assumes that life is meaningless and that whatever we do is ultimately irrelevant or the result of blind chance.

Sadly, Western civilization today has abandoned its spiritual roots and has now morphed into a *post*-Christian culture. I do not mean to imply that Western culture was perfect, or that it even lived up to its Judeo-Christian values. However, for almost two thousand years Western civilization at least *claimed* to be centered on the moral standards revealed in the Hebrew and Greek Scriptures. As a result of our post-Christian age, many people who claim to believe in God don't want to have a real, personal relationship with their Creator.

What Kind of a God Do You Believe In?

Instead, most people want a "genie" in their lives, not an Omnipresent Friend. Much like the classic Walt Disney character, far too many individuals, including many who profess Christianity, Judaism, or Islam, desire a *god of convenience* or outward ceremony. When they are facing a terrible or tragic situation, they want the genie to come out of nowhere and immediately solve the problem. Then when the crisis is over, they want this kind of god to suddenly disappear and go away until they call upon him or her again. In a similar way, many people believe that the major role of God should be as a dispenser of good gifts when called upon to provide them. When they want something, they simply make a "wish" or prayer, and God is instantly expected to provide it. If they don't receive their wish immediately, they lose their faith or wonder if God is dead.

What has caused this warped perception about God? If there is a Supreme Being who controls the destinies of humankind and desires a personal relationship with His creation, then this acceptance into His *presence* comes with strings attached. If He is this kind of God, He has values and expectations for us. This means we have obligations and responsibilities to fulfill as part of a unique and treasured relationship. This is the *part* of acknowledging spirituality that most people today find difficult. They want rewards without the responsibilities. People want convenience without commitment. They want miracles without maturity. People want solutions without stewardship. Finally, they want reliance without the need for a relationship. But the truth is that without a personal relationship with God, we see the world, and our purpose in it, from a very shallow and myopic viewpoint. It is not my intention here to tell you what to believe or to opine about a particular sectarian theology. However, spirituality is an essential element that gives everything else in life additional perspective and meaning. It takes your physical existence to the *next* level and helps you to transcend physical reality and the limitations of your five senses. Don't ignore or minimize the importance of your need for spirituality.

In the fall of 1999, my family and I took some time to attend an eight-day convention in Gettysburg, Pennsylvania. On one of the days, we took a bus trip to tour Washington D.C., and one of the stops was the Vietnam Veterans Memorial. When we arrived I was struck by the solemn environment surrounding the memorial. Shaped like a long letter V and constructed of seventy-four inscribed black granite panels, it contains the names of 58,260 men and women who lost their lives as a result of the complete Vietnam conflict that occurred from 1956 to 1975. The earliest names on the wall are those who died as military advisors before the war, and the last name is for one who died after the evacuation of Saigon.

As we slowly walked up to the memorial, I felt an instinctive urge to touch the names that are engraved into the wall. I had noticed how some people took a piece of paper and etched across it with a pencil to imprint the name of a loved one onto the paper. As we were strolling along the walkway, I dragged my fingers on the wall. I was looking in the opposite direction because I was in a discussion with my friend Tim about the tragic results of the Vietnam War. While looking at Tim in deep discussion, we suddenly stopped. Tim looked shocked as I *rested* my fingers on the wall while facing him. Tim said:

"Stop speaking for a minute and look at the wall."

I continued to wax eloquent about nothing important. Tim said again, more forcefully this time, "I mean it. Stop for a minute and look at the name right above your fingers."

I did, and the name engraved exactly above my resting fingers was: Gregory Thomas.

Now, I am *sure* the cynics and skeptics will say, "Big deal—it is just a coincidence that you stopped there and your name was in that exact spot. You are making more out of this than you should."

If someone wants to believe that a person could randomly walk down the Vietnam Veterans Memorial with its 58,260 names scattered across two 240-foot walls and by coincidence stop, turn in the *opposite* direction, and put his fingers on his own name, that is fine. But I don't have faith in randomness, chance, or luck.

Here is what I got out of the experience: Except for the *grace* of God, that could have been me. If I had been born just a few years earlier, I could have been drafted during those years, and that could have easily been my name representing "me" on the wall. But it wasn't, because God didn't intend for this Gregory Thomas to be on the wall. He had other plans for this Gregory Thomas.

I have no doubt that *my* life has a specific purpose and meaning, and neither should you about *your* life.

In our final chapter, we will look at all twelve principles of this book and see why this is true.

PUTTING THE PUZZLE PIECES TOGETHER

A COMPLETE PICTURE

We have now examined all of the *Twelve Principles*. Together they merge into a complete picture and provide an opportunity for a harmonious and whole life. Let's see how understanding and appreciating the *twelfth* principle magnifies and expands the *richness* of the previous eleven.

Principle #1 is *The Right Visionary Goals*. When you have the added dimension of spirituality in your life, it gives your goals a long-term perspective extending toward eternity. From this viewpoint, your goals not only benefit you today or throughout your lifetime, but they may influence your existence beyond this mere mortal world. You then understand that your goals should be in harmony with spiritual laws and values to be productive and beneficial. You also understand that the personal skills and gifts you possess are not an accident. They were given to you so that you may serve others and make the world a better place to live. A great goal established in harmony with eternal values will benefit generations yet unborn.

Principle #2 is *Continuous Education*. Spirituality helps you to realize that education is not something we acquire only for this physical life. What we learn through good choices and bad decisions is preserved and carried over into a higher level of existence. Our physical existence becomes a constant learning environment and the opening chapter in a never-ending book of life. Spirituality opens new understandings. What we don't know can harm us. As the ancient Hebrew prophet Hosea stated, "My people are destroyed for a lack of knowledge." We press on to grow in knowledge because our desire for education fulfills a greater purpose than can be derived from the here and now. This brings to mind again Thomas Jefferson's words about the value of learning:

> Always leading us to something new, never cloying, we ride, serene and sublime, above the concerns of this mortal world, contemplating truth and nature, matter and motion, the laws which bind up their existence, and the Eternal being who made and bound them up by these laws. Let this be our employ.

Principle #3 is *Maintaining Your Health*. Looking at your health from a spiritual perspective helps you to realize your body is a physical temple, and you have been given temporary stewardship over it. You may have diseases you inherited due to DNA or the environment. You may have even neglected your health in the past. But, starting today, you can value and nurture what you have left. You can respect and honor your body and mind because, as the Book of Psalms states, it is "fearfully and wonderfully made." Being a steward means we accept the responsibility to get enough rest, eat a balanced diet, and get regular exercise. This helps us to be more productive and energetic even into our senior years.

Principle #4 is *Driving Forward*. When you embrace your spirituality, you welcome a life filled with new meaning and purpose. You realize that you were born for a cause and given your talents for an earthly mission. You recognize that daily opportunities are a platform to help you achieve the very reason you were born. When other people abandon or attack a great cause because they lack SQ, you have the drive to go forward even against overwhelming odds or adversity. When you know your mission is right and that you have Divine Providence on your side, nothing can stop you, and you no longer even fear death itself.

And what about the goals you don't reach in this lifetime? You know that it is important to make an effort in the right direction. Even the small progress (or small steps) you have made will be completed in another place and time.

Principle #5 is *Utilizing Your Resources*. As you grow in your understanding of spirituality, you appreciate the incredible potential of the human mind. What separates us from animals is our much greater IQ and the very ability to comprehend SQ. When our spirituality is nurtured, our thinking can transcend the physical senses, and our imagination can grasp concepts we can't ordinarily envision. For example, Sir Isaac Newton was a deeply religious man whose *grasp* of the theory of gravity and three laws of motion were enhanced and stimulated by his spirituality, not hindered by it.

Principle #6 is *Dealing with the Disappointments*. Perhaps there is no greater benefit in possessing spirituality than the ability it provides to deal with personal setbacks, problems, or serious crises. Part of this comes from knowing that there is an unseen hand of Providence ruling and guiding the universe. God is bigger than our obstacles, problems, or disappointments. Things happen for a reason, even terrible things. If we have the proper perspective, we can glean wisdom and maturity from all life experiences. Nothing great has ever been achieved without conflict, adversity, disappointment, and the possibility of failure. Just remember the lives and setbacks suffered by such people as Gandhi, Martin Luther King, Helen Keller, and Clara Barton. They (and many others) are a testament to those who were able to overcome their feelings of disappointment.

Principle #7 is *A Life in Balance*. Taking control of your life and not allowing others or your environment to determine your fate is an important principle. With spirituality as your guiding force, you come to realize that you can have a great amount of control in your life and even *unseen* additional help when truly needed. We have also been given Eternal Laws that will help us achieve a balanced life if they are obeyed. These laws become our compass and the stable foundation of our values. An imbalanced life leads to addictions and obsessions that ultimately will destroy you. As I stated earlier, a productive individual deftly balances personal needs and responsibilities. These include family, work, recreation, spirituality, community, and self-fulfillment. These areas all need a certain measure of attention and nurturing. Spirituality provides the *conscience* that acts as a reminder to keep this important balance.

Principle #8 is *Simple Diversions*. In our workaholic world, we need occasional diversions more than ever. Spirituality reminds us that even though work is important, it is not the *most* important thing in life. Our occupation should fall beneath our commitment to the Creator and our families. Taking time out to regularly enjoy our loved ones, our hobbies, our community, and the natural world provides a vital emotional and social connection apart from the work environment.

Another important diversion that I personally embraced over thirty-five years ago is the observance of a religious Sabbath. For twenty-four hours (one complete day) each week, I spend focused and dedicated time with my family, close friends, and spiritual activities. This is a time set aside for refreshing my mind and getting off the "merry-go-round" of cultural distractions.

Have I received hostility for my observance of a Sabbath? You bet I have. Has it cost me some career promotions or keynote speaking opportunities over the years? Yes it has, but keeping priorities and values are more important than making other people happy. It has been said that people without goals are used by those who have them. I know what my values are, and I am not about to violate them to comply with another person's agenda.

Principle #9 is *Meaningful Relationships*. One of my hobbies is to visit old and abandoned historical graveyards. I have never seen a grave stone with the inscription, "I wish I had spent more time in the office." Actually, my favorite headstone is one that states, "See, I told you I was sick." We tend to spend an entire lifetime trying to accumulate material wealth, prestige, power, or other things that fade with our passing. What really matters is family and friends. If we have spent a lifetime loving and nurturing our personal relationships with others, we leave a true legacy. When all else fails, including our health, friends and family will be there to support and comfort us. Since our *most* meaningful relationships can be with our immediate family and our Creator, spirituality helps us to appreciate that these are intended to last for an eternity.

Imagine sharing a meal and enjoying the company of your great, great, great-grandmother, or an ancestor who lived 2000 years before you were born. What incredible experiences they had and stories they will tell. Possessing eternal life also means you will have the opportunity to have exciting *new* relationships with billions of individuals who lived at various times in human history. Everyone will have his or her own personal experiences to relate.

Principle #10 is *Know Thyself*. I heard a sermon once from a minister who spent five minutes trying to convince the audience how *humble* he was. Unfortunately, you can tell a tree by its fruits, and what he truly was echoed so loudly I couldn't hear what he was saying. Spirituality, when fully understood, arouses a candid exploration of self and all of our weaknesses as well as our strengths. It provides a counter-balance to our darkest thoughts and idiosyncrasies. It reminds us that there are laws that regulate our conduct, and when we break those laws, we suffer the consequences. It teaches us to *listen* to criticism and use it to reinvent ourselves into better people. If our attitudes are right, it points out the "chinks in our armor" and prompts us to overcome our faults and weaknesses. It is also this routine self-analysis that introduces us to encouraging theological terms like repentance, reconciliation, forgiveness, and grace.

Principle #11 is *Passionately Positive*. If a person deeply believes he or she has a life blessed with purpose and rich meaning, how can this person not be greatly optimistic about life? In addition, spirituality makes even mundane, everyday events significant because they are part of a greater overall plan. The past can't be changed, but we can learn valuable lessons from it. Even our mistakes can be viewed as chances to relearn and do better next time. The present is filled with choices that will have a clear impact on the future. When we filter our thoughts and dwell on a positive "can-do" approach to each day, we maintain an upbeat outlook that can help us achieve virtually any goal or desire. When you know you are loved and accepted by the Supreme Creator of the universe, it is possible to accomplish anything.

Do You Possess Both IQ and SQ?

Don't allow yourself to be an Intellectual Cyclops. There is a valid reason why the overwhelming majority of great historical leaders and other great social achievers believed in a higher power that directs and controls the affairs of the universe. It allowed them to see beyond the "now" and inspired them to believe in ideas and missions that would last far beyond their lifetimes. Some were profoundly religious, and it was demonstrated in their writings and public examples. Others were not overtly religious and were not promoters of the organized religions of their day. This includes individuals like Churchill, Franklin, and Jefferson. But it was their deep, personal, abiding beliefs in a Supreme Higher Authority and Purpose that propelled them and their ideas to greatness.

Life can often seem like a giant jigsaw puzzle, and all the pieces seem to be scattered. What is the *force* that can put it all together and make it all work? When I purchase a new automobile, it comes with an owner's manual. When I buy vegetative plants, they come with planting instructions. When I purchase a product that claims "some assembly required," it comes with assembly instructions. Where can we find the owner's manual and assembly instructions for human life? We can only discover it in the *spiritual realm* and in the ancient writings that reveal the Creator's instructions for us.

All of these *twelve principles* are important as they are the individual puzzle pieces that make our life whole and complete. The more of them we appreciate and value, the greater our chances for fulfillment and joy. However, it is this last principle that is at the heart of the completed puzzle. The other eleven principles radiate from it because it gives *additional* depth and significance to each one. I encourage you to appreciate and develop all twelve principles to their greatest extent.

My hope and prayer is that this book will inspire you to *reach* for your personal best!

EPILOGUE

The recurring theme of the *twelve principles* is making the choice to take control of your life. What we do, or don't do, has a profound impact on our level of fulfillment and achievement. By now you have come to clearly see that these *twelve principles* do not stand alone. They are *all* interconnected and fit in harmony and unison. I could spend the next five hundred pages providing numerous examples of individuals who correctly applied many of the twelve principles. However, many fizzled like celestial meteors because they ignored *other* important principles. They come from every walk of life, including business, politics, military, education, medicine, entertainment, and religion. For the sake of brevity, I will only mention one example in detail.

Eliot Spitzer was a rising political star who appeared to have it all and was on a fast-track to great success. Born to an affluent family, he received a superb education at Princeton University and a law degree from Harvard. After earning his Juris Doctor degree, he joined a prestigious law firm in New York. A few years later, he joined the Manhattan Attorney General's Office as a prosecutor. He vigorously prosecuted the Gambino crime family and shattered their influence in the Manhattan trucking and garment industries.

In 1998, he was narrowly elected the New York State Attorney General with the help of a multi-million dollar loan from his father. Spitzer successfully prosecuted cases relating to financial fraud and white collar crime. Cases ranging from computer chip price fixing and investment bank stock price inflation to the 2003 mutual fund scandal were aggressively prosecuted.

By 2006, Spitzer was elected the Governor of New York. Immediately, his autocratic and controversial agenda caused concern, but his influence would not last very long. *The New York Times* reported on March 10, 2008 that Spitzer was a client of a prostitution ring. It had been under investigation by the federal government. Just two days later, he announced his resignation as Governor of New York, citing "private failings." He demonstrated a lack of morality that shamed and emotionally harmed his wife and three children.

He also had committed the same type of crime he ruthlessly prosecuted as a state attorney general.

It is not my intent to go into any of the torrid details of his crime and lack of character. His *legacy* will be to go down in history as an embarrassment to his immediate family and to the office of the Governor. One hundred years from now, the opening paragraph of his historical epitaph will show the deceitful and narcissistic character flaws that brought him down like the *Titanic*.

Why did this happen? The answer is revealed when you look at his life and compare it to the twelve principles. Few would doubt that he had *visionary goals*. He was an ambitious individual who knew what he wanted. Step-by-step, Spitzer walked up the ladder of greater influence and power. He certainly had a good formal *education* from some of the finest institutions in the United States. He appears to have been in good *physical heath,* and Spitzer was absolutely *driven* to be successful in every job he attained during his career.

But, there are *other* essential principles he obviously ignored or abandoned.

He certainly didn't have a life in *balance*. Leading a double life of an upstanding public servant by day and a seedy client of prostitutes by night is not balanced. He obviously didn't have *meaningful relationships* in his life. When you have a truly meaningful relationship with your spouse and life partner, you don't casually betray that relationship. There were obviously dark sides to Spitzer's flawed personality that he never understood or confronted. He truly didn't take the time to *know thyself.*

Is there another important principle we learned that Spitzer failed to respect and appreciate? According to an October 12, 2006 article in *The New York Times* entitled, "Gilded Path to Political Stardom, With Detours":

> Mr. Spitzer is Jewish, but his parents were not particularly religious and he did not have a bar mitzvah; Ms. Wall Spitzer was raised Southern Baptist. The couple celebrate the holidays of both religions with their three daughters but do not adhere rigorously to either.

One can easily conclude from this statement that Spitzer was not an individual who embraced his *spirituality*. Living a materialistic life of deceit, betrayal, and hypocrisy is a ticking time bomb. After a certain amount of time, the bomb suddenly explodes. Within the political arena alone, in only a few months, other recent examples included former presidential candidate

John Edwards, Alaska Senator Ted Stevens, and Illinois Governor Rod Blagojevich.

The message is clear. Each of the twelve principles we discussed in this book are important parts of a complete puzzle. If a few essential pieces are missing, the entire picture is incomplete or distorted.

I encourage you to reread and embrace the twelve principles of personal leadership.

ABOUT THE AUTHOR

Greg L. Thomas has over twenty-five years of sales and marketing experience within the electrical manufacturing industry. Some of his positions have included being a National Sales Manager, National Marketing Manager and Regional Sales Manager.

He also has an extensive thirty-five years experience in public speaking and has spoken to hundreds of audiences. Greg has provided leadership seminars and keynote speeches for organizations as diverse as Ramapo College, FirstMerit Bank, American Society for Quality, Central Ohio Patient Accounting Managers, Shelby County Tennessee-District Attorney General's Office, Academy of Certified Hazardous Materials Managers and the Pennsylvania Governor's Institute. He has also conducted public seminars sponsored by *weLEAD Incorporated*.

Greg has a Master of Arts degree in Leadership from Bellevue University, where he also has served as an adjunct professor teaching courses in business management and leadership since 2002. He is also the founder and president of *weLEAD Incorporated*, and Greg has written articles on the topics of leadership and personal development for various publications. His first book *52 Leadership Tips (That Will Change How You Lead Others)* was published in 2006 by WingSpan Press. Greg and his wife BJ are natives of Cleveland and presently reside in Litchfield, Ohio. His personal web site is located at *www.GregLThomas.info*

 **weLEAD Incorporated** is a major online resource for leadership development. Founded in 2001 as a non-profit organization, it provides hundreds of free articles, book reviews and valuable tips to promote positive leadership values. weLEAD also publishes a monthly online magazine that specializes in personal leadership development and in teaching servant leadership principles to organizations.

Greg L. Thomas and other weLEAD associates are available to provide keynote addresses or workshops for virtually any organization or convention. If you would like Greg to present the *Twelve Principles* to your organization, feel free to contact him at *gthomas@leadingtoday.org*

Some of the additional services weLEAD provides include . . .

- Personal life coaching and business coaching
- Motivational keynote speeches, workshops and seminars
- Management development and training
- Sales training

We also encourage you to visit the weLEAD web site located at *www.leadingtoday.org*

MORE ADVANCED PRAISE FOR
MAKING LIFE'S PUZZLE PIECES FIT!

Making Life's Puzzle Pieces Fit provides sound advice and pages of insight, embellished with a rich variety of anecdotes. His twelve leadership principles provide reliable compass points for earning a living—and living life.

Howard M. Guttman
—Principal of Guttman Development Strategies, Inc.
and author, Great Business Teams: Cracking the
Code for Standout Performance.

An utterly fascinating and well-written book filled with wisdom and insight. Everyone would benefit from reading and reflecting on Greg Thomas' 12 principles of personal leadership.

Michael Lee Stallard
—Author of *Fired Up or Burned Out*

I was personally inspired and energized by the latest book by Greg Thomas. By interweaving seemingly disconnected concepts such as education and diversion, Mr. Thomas was able to provide me with life altering affirmations of balance. The reader of his comprehensive study of leadership principles is well rewarded by the author's personal twist, which not only puts order to life's puzzle but also provides a complete vignette for future success.

I strongly recommend this book for those who wish to become a better leader and those who are prepared to become a better follower.

T.B. Fisher—
Author of *Bought In—Lessons Learned from Established Hippies and Withered Flower Children; and, Why Buy In? —A Survival Primmer for Free Thinkers in a Stereotypical Business World*

"Greg is on to it . . . . Once you know yourself, have decided what your goal in life is and have a PMA [positive mental attitude] you can really enjoy life's fun journey. If you have that special goal in mind, don't forget to form or join a mastermind group.

And Greg is right, 'meaningful relationships' are what make it all worthwhile."

Denis Orme
—founder *www.leader-success.com and www.project-recoveries.com*

"Thomas is artful and comprehensive. He brings to life the keys to personal success like never before. Success is a journey, and Thomas delivers an easy-to-read road map!"

Lee J. Colan, Ph.D.
—Author of *7 Moments . . . that Define Excellent Leaders*

Printed in Great Britain
by Amazon